Cliff Johnson

Putting Down Roots

*A delightful blend
of gardening wisdom,
wit and whimsy*

CLIFF JOHNSON MARKETING
CHASKA, MINNESOTA

Cover design by Roger Kline Graphic Design
Cover photo by Marcus Zbinden

Printed and bound in U.S.A.

Library of Congress
Catalog Card Number: 99-94239

ISBN 0-9670927-0-1

To Wanda,
my wife and life companion,
without whom I wouldn't be
able to spend so much time
gardening.

Minnesota's
Master Gardener Program

The Master Gardener program in Minnesota is an educational outreach of the University of Minnesota Extension Service. It utilizes trained volunteers to assist people and their communities through gardening information and activities. More than 2,000 volunteer Master Gardeners are currently active in all 87 Minnesota counties.

For more information, contact:

Minnesota Master Gardener Program
c/o Minnesota Landscape Arboretum
3675 Arboretum Drive
Chanhassen, MN 55317
http://www.hort.agri.umn.edu/MG/Mastgard.htm

Acknowledgements

All the gardening columns in this book were published originally in the *Chaska Herald*. I wish to thank former editor LaVonne Barac and former staff editor Jenny Eldridge for their initial invitation to begin writing the columns, and to current editor Bob Siegel for his continuing cooperation.

Jackie Smith, veteran Master Gardener and one of the most knowledgeable and gifted gardeners I know, provided valuable assistance with her professional proofreading and always-trustworthy horticultural counsel.

Thanks to Marcus Zbinden, Master Gardener and skilled photographer, for volunteering his photography skills to capture the photo used on the cover.

Good friend and graphic designer Roger Kline created several cover design options, one of which was adapted for this book.

When I couldn't figure out how to configure my QuarkXPRESS desktop software to create this book, Chris Olson and Carol Wierzba of Bang Printing and Dan Rivard of PAR Consulting provided expert technical advice.

I also wish to acknowledge all my fellow Carver/Scott (County) Master Gardeners, many of whom have become good friends and valuable sources of gardening information as we've met and worked together during the past years.

Cliff Johnson
June 1999

Contents

SUMMER

AUTUMN

Winter

What causes an interest in gardening to germinate?

I'm sure my mother — a loyal reader of this column — could recall instances during my childhood when I balked at hoeing weeds, thinning carrots or picking beans.

Has there ever been a kid who liked these jobs?

Despite possible evidence to the contrary, my memories of gardens on our farm are positive. I thought of those gardens the other day as I pondered how a person's interest in gardening develops.

I suspect there's no single common thread — each of us was no doubt influenced by some slightly different set of factors that caused us to want to go out and dig in the soil each spring.

I've also puzzled over why I enjoy gardening while friends of mine with similar careers, lifestyles or hobbies exhibit no interest in gardening.

In my case, being raised on a farm was a natural precursor for gardening because each new season brought another cycle of growth of the farm crops we raised and the vegetables, flowers and trees we planted and harvested.

Our main garden on the farm began each fall or spring when Dad ran the 3-bottom plow through the garden plot just south of our house, turning the soil to a depth of at least eight inches. After another pass with the field disk, the garden was ready for a hand raking and row preparation.

My uncle Vincent loved gardening — particularly flowers — and he was also an adult leader of the Silver Creek 4-H club. That meant we could count on his critical inspection each summer when the 4-H tour visited our farm to review our projects. There's something about 4-H tour that is a motivator for pulling a couple of extra weeds.

2

Like every kid ever born, I remember complaining about the mundane tasks of hoeing and weeding. But I remember more clearly and with more fondness the many fruits of our labor. Early each spring, the rhubarb would push through the ground in April and Mom would make terrific pies and cobblers. We savored the seasonal fruits: strawberries, raspberries, elderberries, currants, gooseberries, plums and choke cherries.

I remember the rows of lettuce, carrots, beans, peas and radishes that were eaten fresh during the growing season and canned for enjoyment in fall and winter. I looked forward to selecting ripe ears from the short rows of sweet corn in our garden; later, we decided it was a lot more efficient to plant sweet corn using one or two of the planter boxes of the field planter.

For 20 years, my wife and I and two children lived on a 40-ft. wide Minneapolis lot. The close quarters didn't permit the luxury of long rows of vegetables and rambling flower beds. Tight spaces taught me how to garden in containers, on trellises and in compact plots.

This period also taught me the value of paying for landscape design. I was capable of some basic plantings, but the professional landscape designer studied our space and inquired about our interests, likes and dislikes. Then he delighted us with a creative plan that combined perennials, shrubs, boulders and ornamental trees that made our cramped space very special.

I enrolled in the Master Gardener training program when my wife and I made a decision to build a new house on a wooded lot in the country. I knew the knowledge gained from the Master Gardener training would be valuable as I slowly and thoughtfully developed the excavated space around our new home into gardens.

Gardening, I've decided, is kind of like a terminal disease... once you've caught the bug, you've got it for life.

We play softball until our bodies complain at age 35 or 45 that it's time to place the glove on the shelf. Gardening, on the other hand, can reward us into our advanced years. My parents at age 85 are looking forward to another growing season where they can enjoy their perennials and annuals, along with strawberries, tomatoes and green lawn.

I like to garden because someone in my past took the time to whet my appetite and stir my imagination for the miracle that happens each year when we grow things or simply watch things grow.

As you prepare to launch into another growing season, think about children or friends with whom you can share this gift. Introduce them to the fragrance of the lilac, the miracle of new leaf buds, the delightful taste of peas popped out of the pod, and the mystery of underground roots.

And then sometime next spring, take a few minutes to sit on your deck and ponder how your passion for gardening originated.

Gardeners reveal their New Year's resolutions

Did you know that 90% of Americans make New Year's resolutions? That's the good news. The bad news, according to a University of Washington study, is that 78% of us fail to keep those resolutions.

Despite that rather gloomy statistic, I am devoting this column to "gardeners' resolutions for the new year."

First the resolutions from some of my fellow Master Gardeners. They resolve:

To resist the temptation of buying more plants than I can get planted that same day. Planting seedlings by the rays of a flashlight is not very intelligent behavior.

To plant more unusual and new varieties...to experiment more, rather than planting the "same old, same old."

To surpass last year's achievement of attracting 10 different species of butterflies by planting and developing additional butterfly-attracting flowers, trees and shrubs.

To convert 2,500 square feet of my lawn to a wildflower prairie.

To convert 700 square feet of my lawn to a perennial garden.

To remove three giant basswood trees and develop this space into a giant flower garden.

To add more mulch, compost and other humus-rich additives to my soil.

To not plant similar varieties so close to each other. Last year I planted six varieties of squash close together, which encouraged disease spread and suppressed yields.

To protect my back from injury by exercising *before* I begin gardening and by practicing more sensible ways of bending, lifting, kneeling and using tools.

To get my annuals into the ground earlier — by late May instead of late-June. My typical pattern is to wait too long, then plant too many plants, which quickly become over-crowded.

To begin my fall clean-up earlier in the fall, rather than finding myself cutting back old growth and cleaning up after the first snowfall.

To landscape our new home and yard with a section of native prairie, instead of seeding every square foot to turf grass.

To not use a ladder when I'm pruning trees. That mistake caused me a broken ankle and shattered tibia that required a 6-inch steel plate to repair.

To plant more apple trees now that I've discovered the formula for producing 3-1/2 bushels of apples from my lone four-year-old State Fair apple tree.

To move my tomato patch to new ground so I can reduce the incidence of blight on my tomato crop.

To spend a little extra to purchase new giant pumpkin seed, instead of thinking my saved seeds from last year will produce a record-breaking pumpkin.

All of those resolutions make perfect sense to me. Now here's my list for next year:

To build more garden elements out of materials that blend in with my natural wooded surroundings. Examples include arbors and trellises made from branches and logs, and walk paths made out of cross sections of logs.

To amend more of my soil where plants are performing poorly. Actually, most soil can benefit from regular amendments of compost, peat and manure.

To plant more evergreens (yes, I know I've advised otherwise in past columns) to attract wildlife and provide winter green. I'll focus on Norway spruce, arborvitae and unusual conifers, and avoid Colorado blue spruce, which is highly susceptible to disease.

To plant more uncommon species of perennials, trees and shrubs. Too many yards are cookie-cutter copies of the yard next door. Best place to get ideas for uncommon species is the Minnesota Landscape Arboretum.

To move plants that are in the wrong place. I'll assess whether present locations are too sunny or shady, too wet or dry. All plants thrive in an ideal environment — the challenge is to create that environment for each plant.

To cut more flowers for bouquets. My summer goal is to have at least one vase of fresh flowers in the house at all times.

Whenever possible, to start from seed, or purchase, award-winning annuals and perennials, rather than settling for the first variety that I come to at the garden center. Look for All America Selections and Perennial Plants of the Year.

To visit more gardens with camera and notebook in-hand. Every garden has at least one good idea we can take home.

Well, I hope you've gleaned at least one or two ideas from this list that you can put to use in your garden. I also hope that you will become part of the 22% of Americans who do, in fact, keep their New Year's Resolutions!

Only one foolproof solution
for this Christmas gift

My topic this week is one of the touchier, more sensitive issues I've had to deal with as a Master Gardener. I decided to write this column as a preventive measure, so the newspaper office won't be flooded with letters addressed to me from perplexed readers unsure of how to deal with this post-Christmas horticultural dilemma.

I'm speaking, of course, of what to do now that you're the owner of a new Chia Pet.

As a Master Gardener, I've been trained to offer counsel not only of a horticultural nature, but also to help you deal with some of the emotional and psychological swings you'll experience as a new Chia Pet owner.

Lest you think I lack the proper credentials, I hastily add that I have owned a Chia Pet, I have raised it to adulthood, and I experienced many of the emotional highs and lows that you now face in the weeks and months ahead.

The emotional gyrations of Chia Pet ownership begin as early on Christmas Eve or Christmas Day as your family opens its Christmas gifts. I mean, there you are, seated between your aunt and a nephew, maybe holding a toddler on your knee. Other people are opening hand-knit scarves, spiffy new toys, Swiss Army knives and sparkling jewelry.

Not you though. Lurking inside the bright Santa paper on your lap is your very first, pudgy, porcelain Chia Pet.

"Oh look at the scarf Billy got — it's beautiful," someone exclaims. This particular gift benefits two people. Billy thinks it's a pretty neat scarf, and Aunt Carol reaps the reward of knowing she crafted one of the nicer garments unwrapped this entire holiday season.

"Wow, look at all the blades on this Swiss Army knife," your nephew beams, and everybody marvels at his good fortune and conjures up images of the adventures he'll have next summer on his camping outings.

And then all eyes are on you as you pull the carton out of the Santa wrapping. "What did you get?" three voices ask at once. Panic sets in. What do you say? You contemplate stuffing the box under your sweater, but this won't make the problem go away.

"I got a...a...Chia frog," you respond meekly. A Chia frog. For Christmas!

Eventually the gift opening winds down and your Chia frog gets momentarily forgotten under your chair. Sadly, your dilemma has just begun. The days and weeks that follow cause your anxiety and confusion to skyrocket.

I am sorry to report that there is a level of fear packaged into every Chia Pet carton. Stated simply, it's the fear of failure. Thousands, maybe millions have failed before you and — even though you've never even owned a Chia Pet — you are some-how subconsciously aware of this statistic.

You're thinking, "What if I follow the directions to the letter and my Chia Pet doesn't grow?" Will this label you a bad person? Will failure to sprout thick green fur (on a frog?) be painful for the chubby critter? Will it bring someone from the Humane Society knocking at your door?

This fear can totally dominate your waking hours and even cause restless sleep. You can be at work and a co-worker may have to repeat your name two or three times before you realize you're being spoken to.

"What? Oh, sorry. I guess I was worrying about a problem at home," you say, not daring to reveal the personal nature of your problem. "It's nothing," you mutter, and try to focus on your co-worker's question.

I've just scratched the surface on what Chia Pet ownership is all about. Crisis counseling may be in order.

As an experienced Chia Pet owner, I can offer only one fool-proof solution.

Soon as you have some private time, pick out some festive leftover wrapping paper and re-wrap your Chia Pet as nicely as you can. Then take it to work with you and discreetly set it on the desk of your human resources director with a note: "For next year's employee gift exchange."

Master Gardener shares her tried & true gardening tips

Each first-year Master Gardener, in addition to tallying 50 hours of volunteer work, has to complete a gardening project and report on it at a Carver/Scott Master Gardener meeting.

In November, Nancy Watschke of Eden Prairie gave each of us a fancy booklet she had prepared entitled "Tips! or Myths?" Her compilation of good ideas deserves a wider audience than just our group. Here are some of her helpful tips.

• Plant your vegetable or herb garden as close to your back door as possible. Your garden will be more convenient and easier to care for.

• Green peppers freeze beautifully without blanching. Remove seeds, chop peppers into medium sized chunks, and slip into freezer containers. The technique works well for onions too.

• To control slugs and snails in your garden, spread sand, kitty litter, coffee grounds or crushed egg shells around plants. Protects your hostas, too.

• Tomatoes do their best in the right company. Preferred garden companions include asparagus, cabbage, carrots, cucumbers, onions, peppers, marigolds, bee balm, basil, borage, parsley and sage.

• Strips of old nylon stocking work great for tying tomatoes and other vegetable plants to stakes because they stretch as the plant grows.

• Use spring-type clothespins to train vines and climbing plants to fences or trellises.

• Stretch woven wire fence along your cucumber row soon as plants begin to bloom. Cucumbers will climb the fence so fruit stays out of the mud and is easier to pick.

11

- Cooking rule of thumb: Vegetables that grow underground should be cooked covered, while vegetables that grow above ground should be cooked uncovered.
- To keep mint from spreading in a small space, plant it in a pot with the bottom cut out and bury the pot in the ground.
- To preserve basil for winter cooking, dry leaves and store in your cupboard in airtight containers. Don't crumble dry basil until you are ready to use it or it will release and lose much of its aromatic essence and flavor.
- Gather herbs in the morning soon as dew has evaporated from the leaves. The plants store up their essential oils during the night; they dissipate as the day goes on.
- Store gladiola bulbs over the winter in old pantyhose. Hang them so air circulates around them.
- When planting bulbs, mix a tablespoon of bone meal in with each bulb. Bone meal provides phosphorus and helps plants develop a healthy root system.
- When planting small bulbs such as grape hyacinth, use an apple corer to dig the holes — it's the perfect size.
- After drying flowers, spray them with hair spray or shaping spray to keep the fragile petals, pistols and stamens intact.
- Placing a coffee filter at the bottom of pots permits water to drain through but keeps soil intact.
- When planting annuals in a very large pot or barrel with drain holes, fill the bottom half with packing peanuts and cover with landscaping cloth. Then fill container with potting soil. Planters will be lighter to move around and you'll spend less on potting soil.
- A simple $10 florescent shop light works best for starting seeds indoors. Hang the lights 2-3 inches above the seedlings. "Grow lights" are expensive and don't work any better.
- Two-thirds of all lawn fertilizer should be applied from mid-August to early November. The other one-third is best applied from mid-May to mid-June.
- Nitrogen fertilizer requirements of lawns are between 2 and 4 pounds per 1,000 square feet. A mulching mower can return as much as 2 pounds nitrogen per 1,000 square feet per year.
- Time your pre-emergent crabgrass herbicide application as

forsythia begin to drop their flowers and just before lilacs begin to bloom.

• Water your lawn when your steps leave "footprints" that don't spring back right away. Water as early in the morning as possible to reduce evaporation. Morning watering reduces risk of disease compared with evening watering.

• Let ornamental grasses stand through the winter for healthier stands of grass and to provide an attractive contrast to the snowy landscape.

• If you see a tree trunk that is flat on one side, there's a good chance the tree is suffering from root girdling.

• Rid your house of mosquitoes, flies and spiders in the summer by hanging bouquets of dried tomato leaves in each room.

• Pests on house plants can be controlled by mixing 1 table-spoon of dish washing liquid with 1 cup of cooking oil. Mix 1 teaspoon of mixture with 1 cup water and spray plants every 10 days.

• A pot of basil set on the back porch will keep flies away from the screen door.

• Keep cats out of your garden by sprinkling a mixture of ground citrus peels and cayenne pepper on the ground. The recipe for rabbits is equal parts flour, dry mustard and cayenne pepper.

• Paint the handles of your garden tools bright yellow so they're easier to find if misplaced in heavy foliage or tall grass.

• Avoid blisters from new wood-handle tools by sanding varnish and paint — smooth, natural wood handles reduce friction that causes blisters.

• Keep shovels, pitch forks and spades free of rust by storing in a 5-gallon bucket filled with oily sand.

• After the last mowing of the year, scrape the underside of the mower deck and spray the cleaned surface with a light coating of WD-40 or CRC-56. This will prevent rusting and add years to mower life. Light coatings of these lubricants will also protect other lawn and garden tools from rust.

• Adding clean clay cat litter to your potting soil will loosen the mixture and add nutrients. It also helps retain moisture and is a good additive for compost piles. *Never apply used cat litter to garden soil or compost.*

• If you cut bittersweet before it pops open (while berries are still yellow), it will stay bright orange for at least a year.

• Attract hummingbirds to your yard by planting salvia, lobelia, monarda, trumpetvine and most other flowers that are tubular, brightly colored and bloom over a long season.

• To attract bees, plant hyssop, catnip, beebalm, lavender, lemon thyme, pineapple mint and lemon balm.

Consider distinctive plants when planning your landscape

I made a statement recently about too many yards being "cookie cutter copies" of the yard next door. My point was that we can make our yards and gardens stand out by their uniqueness and distinctive design.

Each winter I receive a catalog from a Michigan nursery that offers an eclectic array of unusual trees and shrubs. I offer the following ideas from this catalog as a way of stretching your imagination as to the types of plants available to you. Although all the plants listed here are said to be winter hardy to at least -25° F, that's not a guarantee they'll thrive in our Zone 4 gardens. All descriptions are from the catalog.

Tree Serviceberry (*Amelanchier laevis*) — The bush-type serviceberry is fairly common, but this tree grows to 30 feet. It flowers in late spring and produces plentiful fruit for the birds.

Bunge Catalpa (*Catalpa bungei*) — Not named after the sport of jumping from bridges! Produces white flowers with purple dots in July. Native to China and grows to 20 feet. Attracts butterflies and bees.

Sugar Hackberry (*Celtis laevigata*) — The "sugarberry" is a broad, round-headed tree that grows to 60 feet. It produces a sweet and juicy orange-red berry that is gobbled up by birds.

Turkish Tree Hazel (*Corylus colurna*) — From western Asia. Grows a broad pyramidal crown. White flaky bark on younger branches develops into a cork-type scale. Nuts develop in large thick clusters.

American Persimmon (*Diospyros virginiana*) — The American persimmon is the most luscious of all fruits. When fully ripe, the sugar and nutrient levels exceed all fruit except the Persian date.

15

Northern Raisin (*Viburnum cassinoides*) — Considered one of the best fruiting viburnums. Creamy white flowers in late June. Fruit color changes from pink to red to blue to black before it is completely ripe. Was dried and used in the same manner as raisins. Height to 10 feet.

Wolfberry (*Lycium chinense*) — A very vigorous, drought tolerant plant with purple funnel-type flowers and orange fruit up to one inch long. Height to 10 feet with arching branches loaded with fruit. Used in Chinese medicine and said to prolong life, improve complexion and brighten the eye.

Cornelian Cherry (*Cornus mas*) — By far the most palatable of all flowering dogwood berries. Bright red cherry fruit is about 3/4 inch long, tart, and makes fantastic jelly. Bright yellow flowers in early spring.

Blackgum (*Nyssa sylvatica*) — One of the best native trees as an ornamental. Produces 1/2 inch bluish fruit attractive to many birds. Sour lime flavor. Excellent street tree and for naturalizing. Bright red fall color. Will grow in wet conditions or with clay subsoils.

Burgambel Oak (*Quercus macrocarpa x gambelli*) — This hybrid oak deserves to be at the top of the list for wildlife plantings. Produces acorns early, annually and abundantly. Grows to 35 feet.

Burenglish Oak (*Quercus macrocarpa x robur*) — Most requested hybrid oak from this nursery. Grows 2 to 4 feet per year. Produces acorns by the sixth year.

Northern Live Oak (*Quercus virginiana x turbinella*) — A hybrid variety of the famous evergreen oak of the South. Retains its leaves to -10° F or so.

Cucumbertree Magnolia (*Magnolia acuminata*) — Found throughout eastern and midwestern U.S. forests; grows to 80 feet. Indians used it for canoes and bowls. The fruit looks like a red cucumber when ripe.

Umbrella Magnolia (*Magnolia tripetela*) — Grows to 30 feet. Creamy white flowers are 6-10 inches across. Leaves reach 1-2 feet across. In the fall, the bright red fruits look a little alien-like. The bark was used for chewing, which was said to be a cure for smoking.

Ohio Buckeye (*Aesculus glabra*) — Native species of buckeye known for its shiny brown fruit. Yellow flowers in 4-7 inch panicles in May. The seeds are poisonous for humans but relished by squirrels. Height to 50 feet.

Korean Pine Nut (*Pinus koraiensis*) — Produces pine nuts (seeds) about the size of a pistachio. Native to eastern Asia. Tree structure looks similar to a young Austrian pine.

The good news and the bad news about house plants

I have good news and bad news about house plants.

The good news is that house plants are natural air purifiers that absorb and eliminate dangerous gasses from our home environments.

The bad news is that some house plants are actually poisonous themselves, and can be toxic when ingested — a particular concern in homes with infants and toddlers.

Henry Ziemiecki, a Master Gardener from Shakopee, described the good news at a recent meeting. Dangerous gasses enter our homes via a variety of unsuspecting avenues. Formaldehyde, for example, is common in most carpeting, furniture foams and some of our clothing. Plants that absorb formaldehyde include philodendron, spider plant, bamboo palm, corn plant, chrysanthemum and sanseveria.

Gasoline and other fuels, plastics, tobacco smoke and various synthetic fibers release benzene into our home atmosphere. Plants that remove benzene include English ivy, Dracaenas and peace lily.

Another dangerous gas is trichloroethylene, emitted from dry cleaning solvents, paints, varnishes, solvents, adhesives and other chemicals. Plants that remove trichloroethylene include peace lily, Dracaenas, Gerbera daisy and chrysanthemum.

Ziemiecki cited a controlled experiment conducted in 1989 by NASA in which 87% of air pollutants released into a sealed chamber were absorbed and eliminated by plants in a 24-hour period.

How many houseplants should you have to purify your air? Ziemiecki recommends one houseplant per 100 square feet of floor space. So, if you live in a 2,500 square foot home, you should have 25 houseplants, according to this formula.

What about the bad news...houseplants that are poisonous? There are only a few houseplants that are regarded as downright dangerous (if ingested). Two plants are known as the "deadly jewels" — rosary pea and castor bean. You may not have these two plants growing in your home, but their seeds are popular as jewelry ornaments. When the seed is drilled to fit onto a necklace, toxins are released. So, the danger results from beads being consumed by a child who may discover them on the floor or in a drawer.

Two Christmas plants that can cause concern are Jerusalem cherry and mistletoe. The greatest risk comes from ingesting the berries, so hang your mistletoe high, out of reach of young children.

One other houseplant that is generally regarded as fatal, if ingested, is oleander. If you have oleander growing indoors, enjoy it for its beauty, but make sure the toddlers don't sample its shiny leaves. There have been deaths reported from people who cut oleander branches and used them for hot dog-roasting sticks!

One other good news/bad news thing about houseplants is household humidity. Plants raise the moisture level in your home. That's good news if your house is too dry, and bad news if the humidity in your home is too high.

We have so many houseplants that the current humidity in our home is about 42%. When the outside temperature drops below zero, ice builds up on the window glass and damages the wood. Our home atmosphere — thanks to all our plants — is extremely healthy and pure, but it's hard on our window frames when the mercury plummets. To help hold down humidity, we try to remember to run the fans when we shower and we enjoy plenty of fires in the fireplace.

The bottom line is that there are far more rewards from houseplants than drawbacks, so stop in at your favorite garden center this winter and pick out something green to cheer up your home.

Ice, -40° and rabbits still better than armadillo and 'javelina!'

I'll be amazed if anything turns green this spring. If Mother Nature had asked me last fall to write a script for a hostile environment for plants, I don't think my imagination could have strung together the pernicious events of recent months.

The one-two punch of the ice storm and wind devastated trees and shrubs. When the snow melts this spring, the ground in some forested areas, and perhaps in your back yard, is going to look like a war zone.

Then, our week of -30° and -40° temperatures surely blew out the circuits in the delicate cell structure of some woody plants.

And now it's the rabbits. Well, actually, the rabbits have been busy since fall, but I've just begun noticing the extent of their busy work in the last two weeks as I've walked outdoors.

Shortly after the ice storm, I sawed some stout oak limbs that had crashed to the ground during the fury of the ice and wind. This past weekend, I hauled out the chunks I had cut earlier.

As I worked, I couldn't make up my mind if I was better or worse off because the ground was still frozen. Judging by the brown carpet of droppings left amidst the pile of branches and twigs, you'd think it had been the site of a rabbit convention. The ground looked like the bottom of a bird cage. It was like walking on marbles. Thawed ground would have indeed been safer, but imagine my plight had I lost my balance!

Apparently the bark of the twigs and branches that previously had been growing 40 feet above the ground is a taste treat rabbits don't often get to enjoy. Many of the branches were completely stripped of bark.

Closer to my house, rabbits have devoured just about any

every ground-level twig and branch they could clamp their incisors on. Even healthy young bur oak trees have been girdled six inches off the ground. Every needle on several young Austrian pines, planted in September, have been chewed to within a half inch of the branch.

A 20-foot basswood tree with a 2-inch diameter trunk looks like it's fallen prey to beaver. The 1 foot of trunk above the snow surface has been nearly chewed through. Several larch trees planted last spring have disappeared! Even the stems on red twig dogwood have been girdled.

Some of you, I suspect, would contend that these rabbits should have been turned into stew long ago. And perhaps you're right.

Most mornings, several of my floppy eared friends are actually waiting for me when I scatter sunflower seed for the ground-feeding birds. One rabbit held its ground until I got to within 4 feet of it.

Now, I ask you, what kind of sport is it to shoot a rabbit from 4 feet?

Keeping rabbits from devouring my trees and shrubs has become about as big a challenge as keeping squirrels out of the bird feeders. However, as of this week, I'm not going to worry about them quite so much. There are gardeners who would love to trade their pest problems for my rabbits. I know. I read about it on the Internet.

Would you believe that South Carolina gardeners have to contend with invasions of lizards? A gardener of unknown origin is trying to outwit a hungry herd of elk that graze in her garden. Another message laments the work of beaver that are toppling "10-inch diameter oak trees" in her yard. A Texas gardener claims armadillo have completely taken over his garden.

But the number one reason I've decided to live with my rabbits is because a gardener somewhere (another planet?) reports that "javelina" regularly jump her 3-foot fence and eat everything she's worked so hard to nurture.

Given a choice, I'll take rabbits to javelina any day.

Water + sun right formula for a blooming desert

It's amazing what miracles sun and water can create!

I just returned from a week in the desert — Palm Desert, California, that is. And, thanks to liberal daily doses of sun and water, the brilliant colors of thousands of blooming annual flowers delight the eye throughout the Coachella Valley surrounding Palm Springs. Dozens of golf courses and upscale retirement communities seem to compete for attention using the currency of their spectacular flower displays.

We stopped to visit some friends from Chaska who were house-sitting at their son's weekend home in Palm Springs. They had planted tulip bulbs several days earlier and the energetic plants were already up and nearly ready to bloom in the warm sunshine. And to think we'll have to wait a couple of months for tulips to break through our cold earth here in Carver County.

One morning a friend and I walked the immaculately landscaped grounds of the sprawling Marriott Desert Springs Country Club. The view in every direction is like looking through a kaleidoscope. White alyssum and petunias, poppies, pansies and snapdragons in a rainbow of colors are planted in long curving beds, small circular beds, hillside beds, narrow borders and planters amidst a sea of closely clipped, lush green turf grass.

For the week of my visit at least, the Marriott had chosen bright yellow snapdragons as the predominant flower in its overall landscaping scheme. Thousands of yellow snapdragons anchor the center of curved beds lining both sides of the Marriott's miles of paved driveways and sidewalks. The 2-foot yellow snapdragon spires are surrounded by the bright mixed colors of petunia, pansy and poppy.

It's a labor-intensive plan, since my guess is that some other combination of annuals will replace the current collection when their blooms begin to wane.

Water for the Marriott's immaculately groomed golf course fairways and greens and spectacular flower beds is delivered by a precision underground sprinkler system.

If you really want to pamper the shrubs in your yard, you can borrow an idea employed by Marriott for shrubs and other perennials surrounding the hotel and nearby time-share villas. Each shrub (again, there are thousands) is served by its own individual water spigot that trickles an exact daily dose of life-giving water to each plant's root system.

The role of water in this desert community's economy is startlingly evident by glancing across the road from some of the most impressive resorts. There, stretching for miles, is brown desert wasteland dotted with an occasional clump of brown sagebrush amidst the shifting dunes of sand. Add water, and the desert comes alive. Make the desert come alive and sun lovers and snowbirds flock to town.

Two lessons gleaned from my week's stay in the desert (*besides* pondering the question of why I live in Minnesota) are to not overlook annuals, and to create more creative spaces for annuals.

Too often we go overboard planting our flower beds to perennials and forget that, for spectacular color, annuals have no equal.

And second, our ambitious acreages of bluegrass lawns could be a lot more interesting if we dug in an occasional bed of annuals. Yes, fellow gardeners, I'm suggesting that you dig up some of that perfect green carpet in your front and back yard and convert it to oval or circular-bed plantings of colorful petunias, pansies and snapdragons...or your favorite annual.

Oh yes, two more lessons from the desert: Folks there don't get salt on their cars, and they don't spray their windshields constantly with that blue stuff.

Trip to Egypt reveals much beauty in irrigated desert

I am very thankful I live in America.

I just returned from a 18-day trip to Egypt. Many of the sights, sounds and smells of Egypt exceed my capacity of expression. It was a wonderful and unforgettable trip.

Nonetheless, as we turned west on Hwy 494 towards home after a marathon series of airplane flights, I expressed thankfulness for the opportunity I've had to put down my roots in the United States of America.

Egypt has a history that eclipses our country's history by more than 20 times. Recorded history began in Egypt. Its story for most of its 5,000 years is told in the hieroglyphics chiseled into the walls of its temples, tombs, pyramids and monolithic statues.

Egypt is a study in contrasts. As I slipped my bank cash card into an ATM machine on the main street of Aswan, Egypt, and casually retrieved 300 pounds of Egyptian currency, donkey powered carts loaded with sugar cane, fresh produce and crates full of pigeons and ducks skillfully dodged busses and cars on the busy thoroughfare a few feet to my rear.

More than 95 percent of Egypt is as brown as the sands of the Sahara Desert. The other 5 percent is green as a spring lawn, thanks to the life-giving water of the Nile River, which bisects north-to-south the 386,000-square mile country (slightly bigger than the combined area of Texas and Oklahoma).

While we traveled by bus and camel through some of the desert, most of our time was spent in the irrigated Nile Valley, a lush and fertile strip of land which seldom exceeds 10 miles in width. This valley is intensively farmed, often with the exact methods used during the time of the pharaohs. I saw many

24

farmers turning the soil by swinging heavy hoes. In other places, water buffaloes still pull single-bottom plows, and alfalfa for livestock is harvested using small hand scythes.

Fields seldom exceed one-tenth of an acre, but the crops are some of the best I've seen anywhere in the world. The wheat crop, which was just beginning to take on the golden hues of ripening, appeared to me to hold promise of 100-plus bushels per acre yields. To ward off flocks of grain-snatching birds, fields were decorated with numerous scare crows. In many wheat fields, human scare crows sat at corners of fields — an indication that the cost of labor is less than the value of lost kernels of grain.

While most irrigation water is pumped mechanically from the river, I saw quite a few water wheels powered by water buffaloes that take turns walking in circles in two-hour shifts.

With the exception of Cairo, with its population of 18 million, most inhabitants of Egypt still purchase their fruit, vegetables, meat and other foodstuffs at street markets — the action centers in every town we visited. Vendors display and sell oranges, zucchini, tomatoes, beans, bananas, mango, watermelons, fish, goat meat, pigeons and chickens in much the same way that these commodities were marketed thousands of years ago.

The only tractors I observed were pulling wagons of sugar cane to barges on the river. The cane is still cut and loaded by hand, and much of it is still transported by donkey carts. One day I hired a buggy driver to take me several miles away from the river into the fields for a closer look at the local agriculture. We stripped the outer layers off stalks of sugar cane and sucked the sweet juice from the succulent canes. The buggy driver was so impressed with my pocket knife that I had to talk fast to get it back from him.

Most men in rural Egypt wear full-length robes called galibeyehs and draped head cloths as protection from the bright desert sun and to keep sand and dust out of their eyes. After experiencing the wind and blowing sand, I can understand their reluctance to give up this style for western-style clothes.

Purely by chance, our Egyptologist (tour guide) was an amateur horticulturist who is writing several books on the trees and plants of Egypt. Day after day, I soaked in the many nuggets of knowledge he shared on the growing behavior and healing properties of the hundreds of exotic plants we observed. I particularly enjoyed a tour of a botanical garden on Kitchener Island in Aswan.

Mango trees in full bloom gave off such an intoxicating fragrance that I yearned to transplant them in my yard. Oleander, bombax, wisteria, bougainvillea, poinsettia, hibiscus and many other trees, shrubs and flowers were also sporting colorful spring flowers. Date palms were in the early stages of fruit production.

The women in our group were enthralled with the Dolup Palm which, our guide said, is known for its oil that eliminates wrinkles from the skin.

Returning home to cold Minnesota, I wasted little time before rolling up my sleeves and planting dozens of containers of petunia, salvia, impatiens, ornamental grasses, rudbeckia and other seeds. Egypt was an incredible experience, but I'm ready now for gardening in Minnesota.

Mid-March drive down I-35 not all drab brown

You've probably heard the line about the best thing ever to have come out of Iowa: I-35. (My friends in Iowa don't think it's very funny.)

I drive I-35 a lot for my business, and I can assure you that there isn't much happening this time of year, horticulturally speaking, on either side of the Iowa/Minnesota border.

At least that was my conclusion after driving from Chaska to Ames last Monday. Prior to March, this stretch of highway is a border-to-border blanket of snow; in April, it all begins to turn green. But in mid-March, everything from the western horizon to the eastern horizon wears a robe of drab brown.

On my return trip to Minnesota, I decided to look closer for something...anything...that might be of horticultural interest.

Upon closer inspection, I realized that not everything was brown. The woody stems of dogwood shrubs, planted for miles in northern Iowa, have taken on an intense reddish hue that is characteristic of this species in early spring. It's a good reminder that leaves, flowers and berries shouldn't be the only criteria for selecting shrubs. Since our woody plants spend half the year devoid of leaves and flowers, attractive stems can be a smart selection criteria.

Another surprising March color along the barren highway was golden yellow — the color of the twigs of willow trees.

Minnesota can be proud of its impressive stand of vigorous Colorado blue spruce on the west side of I-35 between Faribault and Albert Lea. On previous trips, I've pondered why these spruce look so healthy and full-bodied; this week, I figured it out. The mountains of snow surrounding these trees, blown by the winter's howling northwest wind, will water these spruce trees into mid-summer. It's a nice arrangement — the trees prevent snow from piling up on the highway, and the piled up snow around the trees waters them for most of the growing season.

Farm windbreaks have also trapped mountains of snow. Drifts as high as barn roofs will melt slowly this spring and nourish tree roots well into the summer. There is so much snow in places that planting may have to be delayed in the field rows closest to the windbreaks.

On my return trip, I pondered why trees always seem to get planted in rows. Birds don't plant trees in rows. Trees themselves don't shed their seeds in rows. I can't think of one natural stand of trees in a row. So how come we humans insist on planting trees in rows? If I ever come across a windbreak or shelterbelt planted randomly, I think I'll pull in the driveway and congratulate the planter for his or her originality.

The most curious sight I saw was a stand of 20-foot trees next to a farmstead that had all the bark chewed off from 2 feet to 6 feet above the ground. Since I was driving by at 70 miles/hour, I didn't determine the cause of the damage. Next trip, I need to look closer to see if the culprit was cattle, deer, rodents or something else. Unfortunately, since the 5-inch diameter trunks were completely girdled, these trees will all die.

Another splash of color that contrasted with the drabness came from the reddish-brown leaves still clinging to the branches of red oak trees. Like the red twigs of dogwood, leaves that hang on into March might be a reason you'd want to select red oaks for your yard.

A lot of spruce and pine trees have been planted on the east side of the highway in both states in recent years. Many of these young trees are exhibiting a lot of brown needles — possibly the result of salt damage. When a snowplow traveling 50 mph throws snow (i.e., salt) into a 30 mph northwest wind, the snow (i.e., salt) flies a long way. Trees planted within 500 feet of the highway get coated with this snow (i.e., salt). Let's hope the dose doesn't prove lethal.

What annual flower is planted more than any other?

Looking out the window this morning (Monday...blizzard day), it's hard to imagine that in several weeks we'll be digging our fingers in soil, planting pansies and searching for the lawnmower.

Here's a think-spring quiz: which annual is planted more than any other? Petunia? Geranium? Marigold? Pansy?

The answer is, "none of the above." Impatiens is the most popular annual "by millions," according to the National Gardening Bureau. Next closest rival is petunia.

Impatiens were discovered growing in the eastern regions of Africa, from Mozambique to Tanganyika. They were thought to be native to Zanzibar, an island off the coast and part of present day Tanzania. In fact, the original name was impatiens sultana, named for the Sultan of Zanzibar.

Impatiens were brought to England in 1896 by a British physician and naturalist, Dr. John Kirk. It wasn't until the 1950s that impatiens began being available in individual colors. The two series, 'Imp' and 'Shadowglow,' were introduced in the 1960s.

Claude Hope, "the father of modern impatiens," created a series of eight colors in 1965 and worked with Pan American Seed Company to introduce 'Elfin" impatiens in 1968.

Impatiens are generally available in three sizes: dwarf (8-10 in.); medium (10-12 in.) and tall (1-2 ft.). Most common colors are red, orange, salmon, rose, pink, white, violet and lavender blue. Two types of bicolor patterns are star (solid red outside surrounding white star) and picotee (light color interior bloom, darker at the edge of petals).

In recent years, the variety 'Tango' has become very popular, thanks in part to receiving All-America selection status in 1989. Tango is part of the class of New Guinea impatiens which is taller (14-24 in.), has larger blooms (1-2 in.) and can tolerate more sun than most impatiens. I have Tango growing under lights in my basement and I'm looking forward to watching this variety grow this summer. The color is described as "exotic orange."

If you're reading this in late March, you're about at the end of indoor planting season — impatiens need 8-10 weeks to reach transplant size for setting out in late May. If you don't get them started on your own, don't fret, because garden centers will be displaying dozens of colorful choices at very reasonable prices in just a couple weeks.

Impatiens are an ideal plant for any shady area. They have succulent stems and will wilt quickly in direct sun, especially when they get short on moisture. If you're planting impatiens in a sunny area, make sure you buy New Guinea varieties.

Impatiens in pots and planters are an ideal choice for decks that are shady most of the time. They also do well in window boxes that face north or east.

The best way to select impatiens is to decide on a location and color preference before you walk into the garden center. If you don't give it a little thought ahead of time, you can easily be overwhelmed as you stand facing the long rows of tables devoted just to impatiens. At a large garden center, you may be faced with this range of choices: 15 different solid colors, five colors with star patterns, and three picotee bicolor designs.

An even bigger challenge than selection, however, is finding sufficient "patience" to hang around Minnesota until spring to plant your impatiens!

'Real' gardeners see flowers out their window year-round

I heard Freddie the Gardener (Saturday, 8-10 a.m., KSTP Radio) say that he can actually look out his window in January and see a yard-full of beautiful flowers.

This idea of thinking about — or imaging — your garden year-round is a gift all gardeners can develop. It's why Minnesota's winters are less traumatic for gardeners than they are for non-gardeners. What we gardeners are doing, in other words, is thinking about and forming mental pictures of our gardens every day of the year.

I got a lift the week after Christmas when at least a half dozen seed catalogs arrived in the mail. The following week I was busy figuring out exactly what seeds to order from each, and now it is just a few days until my winter seed-starting gardening season begins. Hey, it's not really winter, right?

Over the years, I've tried starting many different types of flowers and vegetables from seed and growing them under lights from January to spring transplant time. Many of the lessons I've learned have to do with what *not* to do.

Perhaps the biggest mistake indoor gardeners make is planting seeds either too early or too late. The trick is to time your seed-starting so the transplants are at the optimum stage of maturity for setting in the ground in late May.

Some seeds, like cosmos, zinnias, sweet corn and potatoes, don't need to be planted indoors at all. Others, like begonias, should be started in January. Most seed packages indicate the time to plant to achieve this optimum transplant size. I'll start my first seeds this week — begonia seeds ordered from Burpee's. In February, I'll plant impatiens, petunias and geraniums.

31

Many vegetables and larger annual flowers don't need to be started until March, April or early May. One year I made the mistake of planting marigolds too early. I soon had many large plants that took up way too much light space and were leggy and unsightly at transplant time.

One of the biggest challenges to starting seeds is to match the number of plants you start to the light space you have available. Our late-winter days produce too few hours of light to depend on natural light, so florescent lights are essential. Plants need 16-18 hours of light per day. I use four hanging shop lights with double 4-foot bulbs. This looks like a lot of space right now but it will quickly prove inadequate once plants start filling out.

One idea that has worked for me when ordering seeds from a catalog is to select from varieties that have earned "All America Selection" status in previous years. AAS varieties have been chosen by a panel of gardening experts for all-around performance. Some of my favorites are 'Tango' impatiens, 'Purple Wave' and 'Chiffon Morn' petunia and 'Lady in Red' and 'Strata' salvia.

Several other tips will have a big influence on how well your seed-starting project fares. Use a sterile commercial soil mixture labeled for starting seeds. Make sure soil mixture is moist before adding seeds and then cover containers with cellophane or plastic until seeds sprout. I like to germinate seeds upstairs in a south window where the temperature is warmer, and then move seedlings to the basement lights to grow at a temperature of about 65°F.

Seedlings should be watered from below by placing containers in a pan of water. Remove containers when moisture shows on the surface, and repeat watering only when you can feel by lifting containers that most of the moisture has been taken up by the plants. Once plants are growing, it's better to err on the dry side, as containers that are kept too moist are susceptible to disease and mold growth.

If you haven't tried starting your summer garden from seed in late winter, I recommend you give it a try this year. Even if your first attempt is a disaster, you can still visit the garden center in May and buy all the plants you need at the perfect stage for transplanting. Your advantage over other gardeners will be that you won't even have noticed it was still winter back in January and February!

Start begonia seeds now, tomato seeds April 1

The cost of gardening can show up in more places than just your checkbook ledger.

Recently, the cost for me was a week's worth of sneezing and some chapped hands. In December, no less.

If you've been reading this column since last winter, you may recall a discussion about starting seeds indoors. I've found it to be an enjoyable way to extend the gardening season and garner greater enjoyment out of the gray days of February and March.

One of the prerequisites for raising your own healthy seedlings for spring transplanting is starting seeds in sterilized containers. My sneezing began when I brushed out the soil mixture residue in about 500 seed-starting containers from last year. The chapped hands resulted from sterilizing the plastic containers in a bleach solution (1 part bleach to 9 parts hot water). Rubber gloves are highly recommended for this procedure.

The upside is that now I have 500 very clean pots and seed trays ready for new sterilized soil and new seeds.

So here is it, mid-January — too early to plant most seeds, but certainly the right time for ordering seeds and figuring out your planting schedule. Timing is everything because plant species germinate and grow at various rates and you want transplants that are just the right maturity for setting out in mid- to late May. It's a little early to start your tomato plants (April 1 is about right for those Big Boy and Beefsteak tomato seeds), but some poky growers like tuberous begonias can be planted this month.

Gardener's exuberance and zeal often lead to jumping the gun on indoor planting dates; last year I planted marigolds far too early and struggled to keep them watered and healthy under lights until transplant time. My brother — the legendary pumpkin grower from Section 7 of San Francisco Township — started pumpkin seeds this time last year and his plants had about a 1-month life cycle (the latter days of this cycle were not pretty, he informs me).

Here is a partial listing of suggested planting dates for common flowers and vegetables. The numbers and letters in parentheses indicate average days to germination and growth rate for various species (s=slow, m=medium, mf=medium fast and f=fast). So start your seeds accordingly, and next week I'll review some of the cultural steps for starting seeds indoors.

January 15: Begonia (12s).

February 1-15: Pansy (8m) lobelia (8s), stocks (12m), foxglove, violet (8m), celery.

March 1: Petunia (8s), carnations, impatiens (16m), black-eyed Susan vine (10m), torenia (12m), onion, leeks, parsley.

March 15: Ageratum (6m), scabiosa (10m), snapdragon (10m), verbena (16m), Bells of Ireland (21m), dianthus (6m), salpiglossis (9m), vinca (12m), salvia (14m), statice (18m), broccoli, cabbage, cauliflower, head lettuce, eggplant, kale.

April 1: Nicotiana (12mf), nierembergia (12m), annual phlox (8mf), sweet alyssum (6f), tomato, eggplant, pepper.

April 7: Aster (9m), balsam (7mf), celosia (8f), cornflower (8f), marigold (6f), portulaca (8f).

April 15: Cosmos (5f), zinnia (6f), Brussels sprouts, cucumber, cantaloupe, squash, watermelon, pumpkin.

Starting seeds indoors extends gardening season

Starting a few seeds indoors has been the rather modest launch of many a greenhouse career.

It all begins so innocently — a few tomato seeds planted in pots in a south window. Then, next year, a few more seeds, maybe under a fluorescent light. Next thing you know, you're studying plans to construct a 30' x 100' greenhouse.

But starting seeds indoors doesn't have to get quite so out of hand. If you like summertime gardening, starting seeds indoors is a terrific way to extend the gardening season.

Depending on which seeds you choose, your "labor of love" can begin as late as May 1 or as earlier as January.

Although the optimum starting date has passed for some annual flowers, late April and early May are the ideal time to start tomatoes, beets, melons and pumpkins.

While many indoor seed starters have their secrets and special techniques, there is no one best way to start seeds indoors. There are, however, some proven techniques that will help you avoid problems.

Containers — Use only new or sterilized containers that have drain holes at the bottom. I like to start seeds in plastic 4- or 6-pack containers saved from past-year flower purchases. To sterilize containers, soak in a 10 percent bleach solution (1 cup household chlorine bleach/9 cups water) for 15 minutes.

Planting Medium — Soil should be loose and finely textured, well-drained, low in nutrients, and sterile. I've had good success with Fisons Sunshine Mix No. 3 (sphagnum peat moss, dolomitic limestone + wetting agent).

Timing — There's a wide range in optimum starting dates for seeds, and the temptation is to start seeds too early — refer to seed packets for proper timing. Tuberous begonias can be started in January, salvia in March, and melons and squash in late April. The best way to know for sure is to keep a diary from year to year.

Light — For most plants, window light is not sufficient. I light seedlings 18 hours/day with fluorescent shop lights plugged to a timer. Hang lights so seedlings are within 4-6 inches of light tubes.

Temperature — Most seeds germinate best at 70-75°F and grow best at 65°F. I like to geminate seeds upstairs, then move containers to the basement under lights. Keep containers covered with a plastic hood or glass until seeds germinate, then move to lights.

Water/Fertilizer — Water seedlings from below by placing containers in a pan of water. Remove containers when moisture shows on the surface. Since peat-moss soil contains few nutrients, a soluble fertilizer should be mixed with water according to label directions.

Damping Off — This is a fungus disease that attacks seedlings, causing them to collapse and die. Sterile soil and sterile containers are the best protection.

Hardening — Seedlings are too fragile to withstand the shock of moving straight from under lights to outdoor wind and cool air. They should be acclimated gradually in their containers (hardening) by exposing to outdoor conditions in steps building up to all-day exposure.

For more information on starting seeds indoors, pick up the "Starting Garden Seed Indoors" bulletin from your county extension office.

Seed order arrival marks official start of gardening season

How do you gauge the start of gardening season? For me, gardening season begins the day my first seed order arrives. So far I've received orders from both Burpee's and Jung's. I hope you're planning to order and start at least some seeds indoors in the weeks and months ahead. It's a terrific way to extend the gardening season.

Once again, I'll try to grow the new world record pumpkin. I ordered a package of Dill's Atlantic Giant pumpkin seed. I think the weight to beat is only about 1,050 pounds.

I ordered a package of small gold hybrid tomatoes and intend to raise this year's tomatoes in tubs and pots, rather than in the raised bed I've used in recent seasons. Tomato performance definitely deteriorates due to tomato blight when plants are grown in the same space year after year.

I'll be planting two award-winning annuals this year — Prism Sunshine petunia and Victorian Rose double impatiens.

Prism Sunshine received both the 1998 All-America Selection and the 1998 Fleuroselect Gold Medal awards. It is an improved yellow grandiflora petunia "that produces luminous golden-yellow 3-inch blossoms with creamy edges that shimmer in containers and landscape plantings, holding their rich color throughout the summer."

Victorian Rose is said to be one of the first impatiens to produce consistently semi-double blooms "in seemingly endless supply...the flowers are like small roses with old-fashioned rose color, a soft muted shade that combines easily with other plants." Victorian Rose impatiens also received both All-America Selection and Fleuroselect Gold Medal awards.

My 8 foot square raised garden that has held tomatoes in previous years will be devoted entirely to cut flowers this year. I'll plant zinnias, cosmos and some smaller-size sunflowers. My goal is to produce plenty of blooms for season-long flower bouquets.

Another experiment this year will be several species of annual flowering vines planted on an arbor I constructed last fall. The arbor is partially shaded so the vines might not bloom as prolifically as they would if planted in full sun.

One of the vines is hyacinth bean *(Dolichos Lablab)* — "the most beautiful of all ornamental beans...it produces abundant sprays of white-to-purple flowers by midsummer. Its deep purple bean pods and blossoms are edible."

Another vine is cup and saucer vine *(Cobaea scandens)*, "a vigorous, lush climber with 3-inch flowers that open from exotic, balloon-like buds and bloom for weeks to months."

The third vine is asarina Satin Mix, "a stunning vine up to 10 ft. with 1-1/2 inch pink, white and blue bells that bloom until frost."

"Wave" petunias will again be part of my garden this year. Purple Wave, the first of the Waves, has been out for about five years. It was followed by Pink Wave, and this year two new Waves were added — Rose Wave and Misty Lilac Wave.

My order included the two new Wave varieties. Rose Wave is described as "a deep rosy red" and Misty Lilac Wave "produces hundreds of 3-inch blooms in a delicate lavender that fades to silver. It's a color that harmonizes well with almost anything you plant near it."

The thing that's so amazing about the Wave petunias is their ability to spread. One plant can cover as much as 4 square feet and bloom until frost. Past year's experience has shown that Pink Wave is somewhat bushier than Purple Wave, which can get leggy in hanging pots by the end of the season.

Another flower project this year will be two varieties of salvia *(S. farinacea)* — Victoria and White Porcelain. I was attracted by the photo in the Burpee's catalog that showed these purple and white varieties planted together.

Finally, I ordered a package of Dwarf Jewel Mix primrose as a substitute for the shady pots of begonias I've planted in the past. I like begonias but begonia seeds need to be planted in late January in order to have plants large enough to bloom in early summer. I didn't get my begonia seeds planted back in January, so will go with this substitute.

Well, as you can see, I have my work cut out and I didn't even mention all the seeds I've collected from other gardeners during the past year.

Spring

Hungry? Try maple syrup + pulverized corn + bear fat

For a day or two, our mid-March blizzard seemed to put the promise of spring in doubt. Perhaps the winter flannels had been shed too early. But what about the robin that sang to me from the top of an oak tree last week? The chipmunks scurrying around the woodpile? And those swelling basswood buds?

The surest spring signs I've seen so far, however, are the dozens of plastic buckets attached to sugar maple trees just down the road from my house. This annual outpouring of sap signals that these giant trees have broken dormancy and new life is surging inside their rough bark exterior.

What goes on, exactly, inside a maple this time of year confounds even the experts, but suffice it to say that it has something to do with xylem and phloem and a whole lot of built-up pressure. When a half-inch tap is inserted 3 or 4 inches into the trunk of a maple, the pressure forces the sap out the spout into the waiting bucket.

Sap from maples has been harvested as long as there have been maples...or at least as long as there have been squirrels. Although their tapping technique is rather crude, squirrels seem to have a knack for zeroing in on food supplies. Squirrels have been observed gnawing holes in maple bark and lapping the exuded sap.

Statistics about maple sap production are interesting. Maple sap contains between 1 and 12% sugar — the average is 3%. It takes 30 to 40 gallons of sap to make 1 gallon of maple syrup.

The average maple tree yields about 12 gallons of sap per season but some trees produce considerably more. According to one reference, in 1806, 77-year-old John Barney of Guilford, Vermont, made 74 pounds of sugar and 1 gallon of "molasses" from 11 maple trees. In the 1860s, a stand of 100 maple trees in Michigan yielded 950 pounds of sugar in a single spring.

Remember naturalist Euell Gibbons? He claims to have once put six taps in an immense maple and collected 10 gallons of sap in a single day!

The Indians collected maple sap but their tools differed sharply from today's stainless steel and plastic technology. Sap was collected in pans made of birch bark stitched together with spruce roots, then pooled in 100-gallon mooseskin vats and finally boiled down in troughs made of hollowed-out logs. Heat was supplied by repeatedly dropping in hot rocks to maintain temperature.

The Indians used their finished syrup as a seasoning, a dip and mixed with pulverized corn and bear fat as a main dish. By the way, if you decide to try this recipe, let me know because I'd like a taste.

If you prefer a beverage, consider this recipe for maple beer from an 1846 article in The Young Housekeeper's Friend: "To four gallons of boiling water, add one quart of maple molasses, and a small tablespoonful of essence of spruce. When it is about milk warm, add a pint of yeast; and when fermented, bottle it. In three days it is fit for use."

If you decide to tap the tree in your back yard, make sure, first of all, that you have the right species of maple. All maples produce sap but the sugar content in sap from some species is too low to make high quality syrup. The two species most typically tapped are sugar maple (*Acer saccharum*) and black maple (*Acer nigrum*).

To learn more about maple syrup — or if you just want to taste the sweetness of syrup on pancakes — attend the annual Sugarbush Pancake Brunch and Tour at the Minnesota Landscape Arboretum. The tour includes a walk to the "sugarbush" to tap a tree and sample the sap. For details, call the Arboretum at 612-443-2460.

It's tough to grow trophy pumpkins in compacted clay

Chaska's famous clay may have made great bricks but it sure makes for a lousy garden.

If the ground in your garden contains a lot of clay, you might want to do some serious amending to make it a more friendly place for plants. Some clay in soil is okay, since clay contains essential minerals and helps retain water. Too much clay, however, inhibits root growth, is easily compacted, and never dries out. Compost benefits clay soils by encouraging fine clay particles to clump together into larger pieces, improving soil aeration and drainage.

A year ago, I got so frustrated with the clay in one flower bed that I started digging it out and ended up removing 14 wheelbarrows-full before I was satisfied. I refilled the 1-foot deep hole with a more workable soil mixture and this year the flowers have a much better attitude.

It's a lot of work to completely remove clay — unless you own a skid-steer loader, which I don't — so another alternative is to create an above-ground garden by building a planter box out of rock, landscape blocks or wood.

This spring, I built an 8-foot square above-ground "garden" using 5"x6" timbers. I filled the 2-foot high box with about 3 cubic yards of a rich, loose mixture of loam, peat and composted manure. Compared with the clay that lies beneath the box, this soil looks and feels like...well, the real thing.

I planted tomatoes and peppers in this above-ground garden, along with several giant-sized pumpkin plants. I needed rich soil for the pumpkin plants because I'm competing with my brother to grow the largest pumpkin. Last year, I won the competition. He's gotten serious this year, however, and claims his plants are already flowering. I'll have to go over with a flash-light some night and see just what he's up to.

Soil is critical to growing success. Soil not only supports plants but provides the food and water necessary for their growth. Both the structure and composition of the soil affect how much water and how many nutrients your plants get.

Basically, the looser the soil, the better it drains and the more readily the root system can spread.

Pressure from equipment and foot traffic can compact the soil in your garden. Water and oxygen cannot easily penetrate compacted soil to reach the roots of your plants. In addition, the lack of water and oxygen prevents organic matter from decomposing properly. It doesn't take much compaction to affect plant growth. Research studies have shown that normal, every-day compaction can reduce plant growth by at least 10%.

The ideal soil for your landscape is fertile, loose, friable and rich in organic material. Soil containing minerals, a good population of microorganisms and at least 5 percent organic matter is the perfect environment for growing healthy plants, trees and shrubs.

To correct a compaction problem, till the soil and add lots of organic matter. Mix it in good because adding organic material to the surface doesn't help at all if the soil underneath is hard.

Organic matter can hold up to twice its weight in moisture, releasing water to plant roots and improving moisture retention in sandy soils. Remember, organic material is continually decomposing so add more each year to replace the decaying particles.

I'll keep you posted on my pumpkin-growing progress when I've got something to brag about. Meanwhile, I'd like to hear about other giant pumpkins growing in the Chaska area. Write to me and let me know if you've got a trophy in the making. Perhaps in the fall we can persuade the publishers of this news-paper to include photos of the biggest pumpkins grown in this area.

Bountiful gardens begin with healthy soil

A major difference between farmers and gardeners is that most farmers farm to earn a living, and most gardeners garden as a hobby.

Since farmers' livelihoods are on the line each time they plant a crop, they have learned some lessons about how to achieve optimum yields. As gardeners, we can benefit by studying these lessons and applying them to our gardens.

Perhaps the most important lesson we can learn from farmers has to do with soil.

I've had soil on my mind (and under my fingernails) for several reasons. First, I've been digging in my clay again and have had to amend my soil to ensure that the trees and shrubs I'm planting will grow. Also, a local gardener called me last week wondering why her vegetables did so poorly last year. Several questions revealed that her garden has become compacted and has not benefited from any dug-in organic matter for a long time.

The most productive gardens are generally the gardens with the healthiest soil. For plants to grow and flourish year after year, soil needs to have a good inherent structure. Farmers know this, and they work hard to create optimum soil structure for vigorous plant growth.

If you've left your city limits at all in recent weeks, you've no doubt seen and smelled manure. It's that time of year. Two obvious reasons farmers spread manure on their fields is to get the ubiquitous stuff out of their barns, and to add nutrients to the soil.

Another huge benefit of manure, however, is the contribution manure makes to healthy soil. Most manure you see being spread in fields contains high levels of straw or corn stalks that have been used for animal bedding. As this fibrous material gets tilled into the soil, it makes soil much "friendlier" for plant growth.

Soil is classified according to its clay, silt and sand content. The size and proportion of these mineral particles help determine the chemical and physical behavior of the soil. Clay particles are less than 1/16,000 inch in diameter, silt particles are up to 25 times larger than clay particles, and sand particles may be 1,000 times larger — up to 1/16 inch.

Loam soils have the ideal balance of mineral particles sizes. Loam soil contains between 8 and 25 percent clay and is characterized by good drainage and water retention and high fertility.

Clay soils are often highly fertile but are heavy, slow draining and slow to warm in the spring. Clay soil is easily compacted and may bake hard in summer.

Both sandy and silt soils have a low proportion of clay particles, making them much less water-retentive than clay. Sandy soils are particularly light and drain freely; they need frequent irrigation and feeding. However, they warm up quickly in spring and are easily improved with organic matter. Silts are more retentive and fertile than sandy soils but tend to compact more easily.

In a well-structured soil, the particles form crumbs that exist as part of an interconnecting network of pores, through which water, nutrients and air circulate. The structure of the soil determines its ability to hold water, the rate at which it drains, and its fertility.

As you begin to plant flowers and vegetables this spring, study the soil in your garden and flower beds. Have you enriched it recently by digging in generous amounts of organic matter? The best time to amend your soil is in the fall, or in spring before seeding or transplanting.

Improving soil isn't glamorous, but it can do more to contribute to bigger and juicier fruits and vegetables, and more spectacular flowers, than most other gardening tasks.

Planting trees?
Dig a 'basin,' not a pit

In the weeks ahead many of you will be planting trees and shrubs in your yards. I have no way of knowing what percent of tree problems are connected to improper planting method, but I suspect it's a high number.

It's particularly important that we eastern Carver County gardeners understand proper planting techniques, since our trees and shrubs often have to spend their lives growing in heavy clay soil.

I believe the number one tree-planting error many of us make is digging a deep, straight-sided hole without adequate diameter for the root ball. This approach generally results in roots that never penetrate the vertical walls of the hole and instead spend years growing in circles. These plants never develop the root structure to support vigorous growth. It's as though the roots had to spend their lives growing inside a hard-sided bucket.

Horticulturists at the University of Delaware recently completed a tree-planting study that redesigns the planting hole recommendations to promote rapid root regeneration in the surrounding soil.

A planting hole, they suggest, should be dug three times the diameter of the root ball, with sloping sides. This hole should have a backfill volume of up to 400 percent of root ball volume.

A sloped planting hole — shaped like a giant wash basin or bowl — redirects root tips up to the surface where more oxygen is available. The hole should not be dug any deeper than the depth of the root ball. The surface of the backfilled area should be covered permanently with 4 to 6 inches of wood chips or mulch.

The Delaware study also demonstrated that amendments to the back-filled soil (e.g., peat or other organic materials) do not improve tree growth or health. The only benefit of soil amendments, the study found, was in water uptake and retention after watering during dry periods. In other words, the hole can be refilled around the root ball with most any soil as long as it doesn't contain clumps.

Experts name favorite trees
for storm-ravaged yards

Thousands of home landscapes have been devastated this spring by storms. Some experts estimate the Twin Cities metro area lost as many as 20,000 trees.

For many homeowners, the decision now is — what to plant to replace lost trees?

I asked some tree experts what they would plant if the recent storms had destroyed the trees in their yard, or if they were starting from scratch to landscape their yard.

Amy Caldwell, a consulting arborist with Rainbow Tree Care, said her favorite large tree is hackberry, which resembles an elm in growth habit and suffers from few significant disease or insect problems. "Hackberries need some structural pruning when they're young, but they make wonderful shade trees as they mature," she said.

In the evergreen category, Caldwell recommends white fir. She suggests white pine if the site is not close to roads or streets where salt spray might be a threat in winter.

For small trees, Caldwell recommends Japanese tree lilac and serviceberry.

"For a sunny area where there's adequate space, I'd consider the *Acer x freemanii* maple, a hybrid cross between the silver and red maple," said Mike Zins, University of Minnesota extension horticulturist. "These maples grow moderately fast and have excellent fall color." Zins said two popular "Freeman maple" varieties are Autumn Blaze and Celebration.

Other large trees on Zins' list include swamp white oak, sugar maple, black maple, Kentucky coffee tree and sweet birch.

In the small tree category, Zins suggests amur maple, Shan-tung maple, blue beech, thornless cockspur hawthorn, mountain ash and Japanese tree lilac.

Asked for her opinion on small trees, Deb Brown, University of Minnesota extension horticulturist, quickly named flowering crabapples. "They're quick growing and look nice in any yard." Her favorite varieties are Prairie Fire and Red Splender.

Brown also suggests planting three flowering crabs of the same variety in a triangle, rather than planting "one of each" of many tree species and varieties. "I don't like to see yards where they've planted one-each of everything," she said. "It tends to have the appearance of a plant zoo. Grouping three or more of the same variety creates a much more pleasing effect."

For large trees, Brown suggests red maples, providing that soil pH is not on the alkaline side; and river birch, providing that clay soil has good drainage. The leaves of red maple and river birch can get chlorotic (yellow) in soils with a pH of 7.0 or higher, she said.

"Knowing soil pH is critical when selecting trees, and I highly recommend a soil test before transplanting trees or going ahead with expensive landscaping," she said.

An information sheet from Rainbow Tree Care offers the following explanation of pH: "This (pH) is a general indicator of nutrient availability. In slightly acid to neutral soils (pH between 5.5 and 7.2), most nutrients are available at optimal levels.

"Some nutrients, such as iron and manganese, become less available in alkaline soils (pH above 7.2) because of chemical changes caused by alkalinity. Other nutrients become less available in highly acid soils (pH less than 5.5), but these soils are not often encountered in Minnesota."

Another tree-selection consideration is tree size. Large trees provide immediate visual impact but are expensive and slow to establish, while small trees are more economical and will establish more rapidly.

"This quick recovery allows smaller trees to grow rapidly during a time that a larger tree is still struggling to become established, causing the size difference to decrease over time," Caldwell said. Establishing new trees requires 1 to 2 years per inch of trunk diameter, according to Rainbow.

Are some tree species more resistant to storm damage than

others? Caldwell said one trait most storm-damaged trees shared is that they had begun the process of decay. A tree that is hollow or weakened by disease or past storm damage is more likely to blow over in a storm than a healthy tree.

Tree growth rate may also correlate with storm damage. My son, who evaluates hazardous trees for NSP, said fast-growing trees, such as silver maple, seemed to succumb to the wind storms at a higher rate than slower-growing trees, such as bur and white oak.

One final tree list was offered by Gary Johnson, University of Minnesota urban and community forester. For large trees, Johnson suggests Elm hybrid 'Cathedral,' thornless honeylocust 'Shademaster' and 'Skyline,' Ohio buckeye, bur oak, and bicolor oak. For small trees, he suggests Japanese tree lilac and ironwood. Johnson adds that these trees suffered relatively less damage during recent storms.

Two species of trees I suggest not planting in your yard are silver maple and ash. Ash have been over-planted throughout this area, and the limbs of both species tend to be more brittle than other species, leading to frequent injury and branch loss.

Maples can wow you with dazzling fall color

I think the subject of trees should be taught in elementary school right along with reading and writing. I get calls from people who can't tell a pine from a pin oak, and when they go to purchase a tree they make poor choices that they regret for many years.

This is an ideal time to plant trees. If you don't have room to plant a tree in your own yard, ask a neighbor if you can plant one in his or her yard.

A tree is a living monument. Plant a tree in someone's honor or memory, and that tree will remind you — and others — of that person for decades to come.

Now, don't just plant any old tree. There are too many great trees to choose from to waste the effort on a tree that has bad habits (i.e., brittle branches, heaving roots or disease susceptibility).

Select a tree that will satisfy your objectives and fit your space. Search out the tree specialist at your favorite reputable garden center. Tell him or her where you want to plant the tree (in sun or shade, north or south side of house, wet or dry soil, etc.), and what qualities you're expecting from a tree (fall color, shade, appeal to wildlife, etc.).

One tree family that offers a great deal of variety — and can be quite confusing — is the maple. To avoid mistakes, you almost have to use botanical (genus + species) names. No two nurseries label their stock alike, so it's best to go armed with some prior knowledge. For the maples listed below, I've included both the common and scientific names.

Sugar Maple *(Acer saccharum)* — The maple most people think of first, and the source of maple syrup. Sugar maples can grow to 65 feet and show off dazzling red, orange and yellow fall color. If you have room for a sugar maple, consider the cultivars "Majesty," "Green Mountain" or "Legacy."

Silver Maple *(Acer saccharinum)* — Fastest growing of all maples, to a mature height of 75 feet. Not a good front or back yard tree because it has brittle branches and vigorous roots that can heave sidewalks and disrupt lawns.

Red Maple *(Acer rubrum)* — Grows to 60 feet and boasts outstanding red fall color. Red maples like full sun and slightly-acid, moist soil. Select a variety from a northern seed source; best bets are "Northwood," "Olson" and "Autumn Spire."

Freeman Maple *(Acer x freemanii)* — A hybrid cross of silver and red maple that combines the good color of red maple with the fast growth of silver maple (but without the above-ground roots and brittle branches). Grows to 40 to 60 feet. The most-popular variety is "Autumn Blaze."

Norway Maple *(Acer platanoides)* — A strong-branched tree that provides dense shade. Some varieties have red or purple leaves early, which turn green in summer. Fall leaf color is usually yellow. Grows to 40 to 60 feet. Good choices are "Deborah" and "Emerald Queen."

Amur Maple *(Acer ginnala)* — Can be grown as small tree or multi-stemmed hedge. Grows to 15 to 18 feet. Brilliant orange-crimson fall color. Some varieties have showy fruits (seeds) in summer/early fall which add interest but can be annoying on a manicured lawn.

Tatarian Maple *(Acer tataricum)* — Very similar to amur maple; grows to 25 feet. Both tatarian and amur maples are good trees for planters and patios.

Boxelder *(Acer negundo)* — Yes, a boxelder is a maple. But don't plant one...pick one of the maples listed above.

Most people like maples for their fall color. For this reason, you might want to wait until fall to plant a maple. Then you can browse a nursery and pick the tree with the best color. But even that's not a sure thing; my father and I once selected a dazzling red/orange-leafed sugar maple out of a woods and planted it in my front yard. For the next 15 autumns, it turned from green to pale yellow to drab brown.

Remember that maples are susceptible to sun scald injury on

the south and southwest sides of the trunk in winter. The bark heats up during mid-day, then cools quickly when the sun sets, resulting in vertical splits in the trunk bark. To help prevent sun scald injury, wrap trunks with tree wrap in late fall and remove it in April.

1998 spring rivals 1987 and 1977 as earliest on record

How "early" is this spring? One of the very earliest, based on records from previous springs.

Perhaps the earliest spring during this half century was 1987. Greg Spoden, a climatologist with the Department of Natural Resources, told me that Lake Minnetonka's ice in 1987 left the lake on March 21, compared with April 3 this year. Average April temperature in 1987 was 53.5°F, compared with 50.6°F this year. The 1986-87 winter (Dec-Jan-Feb) averaged 21.7°F, compared with 21.9°F this year.

Another early spring occurred in 1977. I enjoyed reading about the 1977 spring in Jim Gilbert's Nature Notebook. Here are some of his notes from that spring, and my comparisons from the same days this April:

Jim Gilbert/April 26, 1977 — We normally look for the first common purple lilac flowers and first crabapple blossoms in mid-May, but both started blooming today. Forest areas are quite shady now that leaves have reached about one-third their mature size. Violets and wood anemone are in full bloom. Bees are buzzing around and visiting the fragrant white flowers of native American plum trees. Virginia creeper is leafing out.

Cliff Johnson/April 29, 1998 — I observed all of these early signs today in my yard and the surrounding woodland.

Jim Gilbert/April 30, 1977 — Ever since I began taking notes on plant development 10 years ago, this is the earliest spring I have recorded. Professor A. C. Hodson's (a University of Minnesota naturalist) 30-year record from 1941-70 points out that the spring of 1946 was the earliest he had recorded, but in looking through his records, I see that spring 1977 is even earlier.

A few entries from my Arboretum field notes provide more

examples of how early spring is today: Sugar maples have finished blooming, seeds are forming and leaves are half way out. Bur oaks are blooming, and leaves are about one-fourth their mature size. Eastern redbuds have starting flowering.

Cliff Johnson/April 30, 1998 — That is precisely where my sugar maples, bur oaks and eastern redbuds are in development.

One of the joys of spring is the element of surprise. I was pleasantly surprised at nearly every step and turn during April and early May. One of those surprises occurred as I made a delightful discovery.

Two years ago, my son Fletcher (a forestry major) planted upwards of 150 Ohio Buckeye tree seeds on our mostly wooded lot. Last spring and summer, he searched in vain for Ohio Buckeye seedlings and we concluded the ubiquitous squirrels had dug all the seeds as a delicious taste treat.

A couple of weeks ago, I discovered an unusual 8-inch plant growing in a patch of pachysandra in my back yard. At first I wasn't sure what this multi-leafed plant was. Later, I was walking in another part of my lot and noticed two more identical plants. Then I realized these were Fletcher's Ohio Buckeyes!

Now they seem to be appearing all over. At last count, I've found 23 Ohio Buckeye seedlings. I'll have to move several away from my flower gardens, but most can stay right where Fletcher planted them.

What's an Ohio Buckeye? Its botanical name is *Aesculus glabra* and it's native to the Midwest and hardy in Zones 3 to 7 (we're in Zone 4). It has handsome and somewhat unusual leaves (5-7 leaflets per 6-inch leaf) and 2-inch seeds in the fall that are prized by squirrels.

Ohio Buckeye can grow to 80 feet but are not recommended as a yard tree because of the litter they produce and the problem of leaf scorch in late summer. Fletcher assures me the seeds he planted are resistant to leaf scorch because he picked them from the same "mother tree" that the University uses for propagation, and this tree has always been resistant to leaf scorch.

One of my greatest challenges this spring has been to practice patience. Based on the daily weather pattern, it felt like annuals could have been set outside in mid-April. The big question was whether frost would occur before the traditional "safe" date of May 15-20. On May 1, I finally gave in and potted a number of annuals started from seed in March with full recognition that frost was still possible. As of this writing (May 15), frost seems highly unlikely, so annuals can be set out. It turns out that annuals could have been set out in April! Most tender annuals don't put on much top growth during the first several weeks, but the roots begin developing and growth really takes off when night-time temperatures warm.

Several reminders: Don't prune oak trees until after August 1 to prevent infection from oak wilt disease. We'll just have to cross our fingers concerning oaks that were accidentally pruned by Friday's storm.

Also, watch your white birch trees for birch leafminer infestations, and spray trees that exhibit more than 30 percent infestation. Keep an eye on your spruce and pine for sawfly larvae. And follow all label directions when handling any chemicals.

Select award-winning varieties for best gardening results

Fast-forward your mind...you're in the garden center, it's elbow-to-elbow people, and the display tables are crammed with hundreds of flats of young plants.

Will you select varieties that are proven performers, or will you settle for whatever's the cheapest, closest to your shopping cart, or appears to have the prettiest blooms?

I've mentioned All-America Selections and Perennial Plants of the Year before in this column, and I highly recommend looking for these designations when ordering seed or buying plants this spring.

Prior to 1932, there were no industry standards for evaluating plants and flowers. This led to problems of questionable improvement of new varieties, inadequate seed supplies for new varieties, and biased variety testing. The AAS was formed to solve these problems.

AAS judges compare and rate new plants and cultivars with the industry's best. Only those new plants deemed superior are given the coveted AAS award.

The judges are volunteers from the seed industry, universities and botanical gardens throughout the U.S. and Canada. Since they don't know the original source of the seed and do not score their own entries, they remain impartial. Their evaluations are based on color, disease resistance, insect and weather tolerance, uniformity, uniqueness, fragrance and, for vegetables, flavor, texture and productivity.

Most seed catalogs will include the AAS symbol somewhere in the variety description, and it may also appear on the plastic stake inserted in trays of AAS seedlings.

Perennial Plants of the Year are selected by the Perennial

Plant Association. You can't go wrong planting one or more of these Perennial Plants of the Year:

1998: Echinacea purpurea 'Magnus'
1997: Salvia x 'May Night'
1996: Penstemon digitalis 'Husker Red'
1995: Perovskia atriplicifolia
1994: Astilbe x 'Sprite'
1993: Coreopsis verticillata 'Moonbeam'
1992: Veronica x 'Sunny Border Blue'
1991: Heuchera micrantha 'Palace Purple'
1990: Phlox divaricata

While I'm on the subject of picking and planting winners, here are the "best bet" annuals from the 1996 annual flower trials at the University of Minnesota Morris experiment station:

Marigold: Antigua Yellow
Alyssum: Cheers White, Wonderland White,
Melampodium: Medallion
Petunia: Purple Wave, Heavenly Lavender, Merlin Pink, Pink Storm, Rose Madness.
Rudbeckia: Indian Summer
Salvia: Reference, Silver, Victoria
Snapdragon: Liberty Crimson
Verbena: Quartz Scarlet
Zinnia: Short Stuff Orange

If you want to be as trendy in your neighborhood as Martha Stewart is in her's, you'll want to plant "mesclun" this spring. Mesclun is the name for "designer greens" that are the rage for health-conscious Americans. Mesclun, an import from France, refers to tender young lettuces and other greens that are low in calories, high in nutrition, and very tasty.

Traditional French mesclun calls for chervil, arugula, lettuce and endive in precise proportions. You may come across seed mixes that include lettuces (Bibb, Romaine, oakleaf and crisphead), arugula, endives, mustards, purslane, chicory, cresses, parsleys, fennels, escarole, and tender wild greens.

Many gardeners choose to pick mesclun just before the meal, serving it simply with only a bit of light vinaigrette dressing. Mesclun can also be stir-fried or wilted in butter and served with fresh vegetable dishes or pastas.

Early spring guidelines for growing a healthy lawn

This week is a good time to think about your lawn. Notice I said "think" about your lawn, not "do" your lawn. If you're reading this in mid-April, it's likely still too early to walk on your lawn, mow your lawn or fertilize your lawn.

Walking on your lawn in early spring when the ground is soft and moist can compact the soil so grass roots are robbed of oxygen. Test your lawn — if your feet sink in even a little, try to stay off it for a couple of extra days.

If your lawn is too wet to walk on, it's definitely too wet to rake. Raking turf that's too wet will pull up roots and do more damage than good.

Don't be too eager to fertilize your lawn. Grass should be allowed to come out of dormancy slowly. Early in the growing season, grass is involved in the activity of reproduction, not growth. Fertilizing during April or early May can actually stress your grass and encourage more vigorous growth of weeds. Best advice for getting an early spring start on lawncare is to fertilize and rake it in the fall, and let it care for itself in the spring (a lot of good that advice does you now, you're probably thinking...).

A general thumbrule for fertilizing turf grass is to apply two-thirds of the year's fertilizer from mid-August to early November, and the other one-third between mid-May to mid-June.

Many lawn lovers like to combine crabgrass control and fertilizing into one operation. Best timing for crabgrass control is when Forsythia begins to drop its flowers and just before lilacs begin to bloom — usually May 10-20.

Unlike quack grass and some other pesky lawn "enemies," crabgrass is an annual. It sprouts and grows each year from seed. The crabgrass chemical you apply kills crabgrass as it germinates and should be applied several weeks ahead of germination, which begins in late May or early June.

If you are intending to sow grass seed to establish a new lawn or fill in bare spots in an existing lawn, early spring is an excellent time for this activity. Newly seeded areas need to be kept moist until grass seed sprouts. Water the seeded area two or three times daily until seed germinates. You can cover the surface area lightly with straw to keep the soil surface moist. After seedlings appear, begin watering less frequently but for longer periods until grass is well established.

When you enter the garden center to purchase grass seed, don't just grab the first container of seed you see on the shelf. Consider the location where you intend to seed, and purchase the right seed based on these situations:

FULL SUN: For high-management/high-wear areas, look for a blend containing 50-75% improved Kentucky bluegrass and 25-50% improved perennial ryegrass. For low-management/low-wear locations, use a blend of 60-75% Kentucky bluegrass (mixture of common and improved), 25-40% fine-leaf fescue, and 5-15% improved perennial ryegrass.

FILTERED SHADE: Look for a blend containing 50-60% fine-leaf fescue, 40-50% Kentucky bluegrass, and 5-10% improved perennial ryegrass.

HEAVY SHADE: Choose either a blend containing 80-85% fine-leaf fescue and 15-20% Kentucky bluegrass or a blend of 80-85% fine-leaf fescue + 5-10% *Poa trivialis* + 5-10% Kentucky bluegrass.

PLAY/ATHLETIC AREAS: Plant a blend of 50% Kentucky bluegrass and 50% perennial ryegrass.

Finally, if you rake and bag your grass clippings after mowing, consider scattering the clippings on your lawn. New lawn mowers do an excellent job of fine-cutting and distributing mown grass. These grass clippings can add up to 1 pound of nitrogen per year to your lawn — one-third of your lawn's annual requirement — and it's free fertilizer.

Crabgrass control, pruning flowering shrubs, and winterkill

I've received many calls recently about crabgrass control in lawns, winterkill, and pruning trees and shrubs. First, the crabgrass.

Crabgrass is a warm-season annual grass which grows best in the heat of mid-summer. Crabgrass overwinters as seed, comes up about mid-May or later, and is killed by fall frosts.

The best control for crabgrass and other weeds is a healthy, dense, vigorous lawn of Kentucky bluegrass and fine-leafed fescue. Another natural defense against crabgrass is to not mow grass too short. Mowing at 3-inch heights provides more shade at soil level, which reduces the ability of crabgrass to germinate.

If a pre-emergence week killer is used to kill crabgrass seedlings as they germinate, it needs to be applied during the first two weeks of May. One application should provide season-long control. Always follow label directions, which usually specify applying 1/4 to 1/2 inch of water after application to move granules to the soil surface.

Be wary of lawn services that tell you your lawn needs five or more fertilizer applications. The most your lawn needs to be fertilized is three times per year, and two of those applications should be in early and late fall. Most lawns can get by with an application of fertilizer in late spring and another in the fall.

❖

There is no one time of the year to prune ornamental shrubs. Timing is most dependent on when a shrub flowers and whether it flowers on old wood or new wood. Old wood is wood that has gone through at least one winter; new wood is the part of the branch that has grown in the current growing season.

Shrubs that bloom early in the growing season on old wood (azaleas, forsythias, lilacs and Juneberries) should be pruned immediately after they finish blooming.

Shrubs that flower later in the year on old wood (mockorange, potentillas, roses and weigela) should be pruned before growth starts in the spring or after blooming.

Shrubs that flower on new wood (clematis, Annabelle and PeeGee hydrangeas, Anthony Waterer spirea) should be pruned before the growing season begins. Prune these shrubs to the first pair of buds above the ground.

Fruit-bearing shrubs like barberry, buckthorn, dogwood, honeysuckle and viburnums should all be pruned in the spring before growth starts.

The best way to prune most shrubs is to completely remove the oldest one-third of branches each year. Removing the entire branch is better than just trimming the tips because it allows leaves to grow throughout the entire plant. Removing just the tips around the entire shrub causes overgrown plants that have leaves only on the outer branches and remain bare in the center.

Junipers, arborvitae, and yews can be pruned at any time, although early in the growing season is best. Evergreen shrubs in the pine family (e.g., Mugo pine) can only be pruned when they are at their candle stage in the spring. These candles, or new growths, can be cut back by one-third to one-half their length. Cutting past the candle or pruning at the wrong time will result in dead stubs.

❖

Once again this spring, many pines, spruce, yews, and arborvitae are exhibiting a lot of brown from winterkill. Keep an eye on the brown areas this spring. If no green growth occurs by June, this part of the plant is most likely dead and will need to be removed. Some needles that are still partially green may recover once juices began flowing within the plant.

The best prevention against winterkill is to plant hardy varieties in the first place, and then to mulch young trees and shrubs in the fall, keep plants well watered right up until the ground freezes, and avoid fertilizing plants after the first week of August (to discourage late-season growth spurts).

A lawn is just one idea for your yard

Seems like I spent most of my youth mowing the lawn. It was hotter then, I think, and the grass grew faster than it does nowadays. Plus, we didn't have a riding lawn mower.

We had a pretty good-sized lawn, but it wasn't a five-acre field like some lawns I see today. There definitely is a correlation between large lawns and the advent of the riding lawnmower. (In the "old days," the correlation for a large lawn was the number of kids in the family!)

I think another motive for large lawns is that idyllic picture in a parent's or grandparent's mind of the whole clan out there on that grand expanse of green playing a multi-generational game of softball.

When I see a large lawn, my imagination runs wild with images of what could be planted or placed in that lawn area. Things like trees. Shrubs. Patios. Perennial gardens. Wildflowers. Ponds. Rock gardens. Orchards.

If a large lawn is your pride and joy, my advice is to not change a thing. But if you occasionally ponder alternative uses for the space outside your window, here are some ideas. (NOTE: Since readers' "yards" may vary in size from an apartment windowsill to a 1,000-acre farm, not every idea will fit each person's space.)

The first step is a plan. Ask yourself how you want to use the space, and what types of materials you find most appealing. A landscape plan can incorporate a variety of objects — large and small plants, wood, rock, etc. A plan can be informal or formal; it can include your own ideas as well as ideas from friends, neighbors and gardens you've seen elsewhere.

I believe a formal landscape plan created by a landscape

designer is a sound investment. Reputable landscape designers have creative ideas that can be tailored to your space and tastes.

I have had several plans created by landscapers, with excellent results. For many years I lived on a 40'x120' lot that surrounded a two-story house. Despite the limited yard area, we were able to create a nice landscape that incorporated 14 tons of rocks (6-inch to 2-foot diameter), evergreen and deciduous trees and shrubs, annual and perennial flowers, planter boxes, hanging pots, a small patio and deck, and a contoured lawn. A medium-height fence on both sides defined the space and provided a backdrop for plantings.

Think of your yard as art. You can alter the picture quite dramatically or "just a little bit" depending on the materials and plants you choose and the way you combine them.

If you have existing trees, consider planting woodland shrubs and wildflowers to create a woodland garden. Many wildflowers bloom in the spring before the leaves emerge, and then ferns, hostas and other shade-loving plants emerge and thrive under the shade of larger trees.

If you have lots of space, consider establishing a "prairie garden" by planting native prairie grasses and perennials. Check out the Minnesota Landscape Arboretum's excellent prairie area to determine if a prairie garden appeals to you. An alternative to a native prairie is to plant prairie plants in flower beds (e.g., Blazing star, Kansas gayfeather, blanket flower, butterfly weed).

For smaller yards, rock or wall gardens can offer visual diversity and provide an environment for interesting shrubs and flowers. Rock and wall gardens work best in yards that have some natural slope.

Flower gardens with curving borders are more pleasing to the eye than straight-edge borders. You can add interest with fence backdrops, boulders, trellises, arbors, benches or other objects. Select a mixture of flowers so something is in bloom from early spring to late fall.

Yards and gardens are an expression of your personality and lifestyle. It all comes down to creating a space that you enjoy. For some that space may be a lush lawn where all the blades of grass point in the same direction.

Really hot water best treatment for poison ivy

I've got poison ivy. Again.

I think this is my sixth or seventh case of poison ivy since moving to my present home site — I've lost count.

My first case was the most severe. For a week, my wrists and forearms looked like boiled rhubarb. That episode began with a day of brush clearing to prepare the site of a mound septic system. Not having reacted to the disease before, I didn't pay much heed to poison ivy amongst the hundreds of small trees that had to be cut and hauled away. The exposed skin between my tee-shirt sleeves and gloves really took a hit.

Since then, I've avoided the thickest stands of poison ivy in the areas that aren't being converted to gardens, and sprayed with Roundup other areas situated where I want to grow flowers, lawns and other plants.

My current outbreak is only on my hands, and it's a humdinger. A couple of weeks ago, I planted dozens of perennial plants in a shady garden-to-be beneath a giant basswood tree. Previously, this space was a tangle of prickly ash, gray dogwood, plum and poison ivy. I removed everything above ground but obviously didn't respect the poisonous roots in the soil.

Late in April, this space *looked* pretty harmless. None of the previous woody plants and weeds had sent forth their tender new spring shoots and the soil looked so inviting.

As I dug holes for each precious bare-root perennial that had just been delivered by UPS, I snipped away at the maze of criss-crossing roots and pulled them out with my hands. Not a smart move. The deadly poison ivy oil accumulated on my hands, and a potent dose must have lodged underneath my

69

wedding ring because that finger currently looks like uncooked meatloaf (I washed my hands in the days ahead, but never removed and scrubbed the ring!).

Everybody reacts differently to poison ivy. My son helped me clear brush that earlier time and never had a problem. My dad once burned a brush pile and inhaled the smoke from burnt poison ivy and paid a stiff price by getting poison ivy in his throat and lungs.

The poison found in poison ivy is urushiol (actually four poisons that differ in minor chemical ways). A Minnesota Extension Service booklet, "Pesky Plants," says that we are initially immune to poison ivy but our sensitivity increases over time from repeated exposures.

Non prescription hydrocortisone creams or lotions may reduce irritation but I have found the best treatment is running the affected area under hot water for as long as I can stand the heat. The feeling of hot water pouring over the blisters is one of the most soothing feelings I have ever experienced and it relieves the itch for several hours.

Now, you might ask, what kind of darn-fool gardener would dig in dirt containing poison ivy roots without wearing gloves? Me for one, I guess. While gloves may work for you, they get in my way. It's hard to separate tender roots of bare-root perennials with the thick, non-feeling fabric of gloves. And what about the future use of those gloves? Would you wear a pair of gloves again if you knew they were smeared with the pernicious oil of poison ivy?

So, it seems to me, I've got two choices.

I can quit going outside, and avoid poison ivy for the rest of my life.

Or I can continue gardening and expect to encounter the red, itchy blisters from time to time, which will provide interesting fodder for some future column.

Besides, it feels so good to run my blisters under really hot water.

Oak wilt...frost damage...or some new mystery disease?

I stood belly to belly with a 150-year-old bur oak tree *(Quercus macrocarpa)*, craning my neck to search its lofty limbs and branches for the slightest sign of life. Think about it — this creature of habit had been doing its leaf thing for more springs than Minnesota has been a state!

Bur oaks grow slowly (1 inch of trunk diameter every 12 years) and are not easily transplanted, which explains why so few are selected by homeowners as back yard shade trees. Very old bur oaks can live for 300 years and reach 100 feet in height.

On this spring day — a spring certainly no better or worse than many before it — the bur oak in my yard stood motionless, its branches and twigs as bare as my bald head. Was it dead? No, because several yellow-green clusters of new leaves were managing to push through their terminal bud cases on branches close to the ground. Was it dying? It certainly looked that way.

Elsewhere on my lot, and scattered throughout the adjoining golf course, other less-majestic bur oaks were also struggling to send forth their spring robe of green.

My initial suspicion was depressing — just about more than a grown man can bear: Oak wilt. Had this deadly epidemic spread underground through the interconnecting root systems of all of these brothers and sisters and first cousins?

Oak wilt has been killing Minnesota oak trees since the late 1800s. Red oaks can succumb in a single season, while white and bur oaks may take up to five years to die. Oak wilt is caused by a sapwood-inhabiting fungus which is directly related to the fungi that cause Dutch elm disease. Disease transmission is most common through the roots but can also be spread by picnic beetles in the spring via wounds in a tree's bark.

I called DNR forester Al Olson, who offices in Waconia and watches over the forests of Carver, Scott and Hennepin counties. He stopped by later that afternoon and crawled around the upper limbs of one of my bur oaks, studying the bare twigs and cutting a few samples. He left scratching his head, somewhat puzzled by the situation, and promised to call in a couple of days when the lab results are complete. In recent days, Olson said, he had heard about similar problems with bur oaks in Plymouth and in Credit River Township in Scott County.

Several phone calls from homeowners the next day left me perplexed. Some of the callers reported oak leaves failing to appear, while others asked about barren ash and poplars. A drive to Chaska revealed other stands of equally aged bur oaks with the same problem.

I called Cindy Ash, University of Minnesota plant pathologist, to get her fix on the problem. "I doubt you've got oak wilt," she said quickly. "More likely, your trees all suffered bud damage on April 5, when the temperature dropped to -8° F. It was particularly damaging to oaks and poplars."

My spirits rose as she spoke. Frozen terminal buds meant a momentary set back — not death, as in forever. Frozen terminal buds meant that leaves might still be forthcoming from lateral buds present on all branches.

I called Olson again, sharing this new diagnosis. "That makes more sense than oak wilt," he said. "I've seen oak wilt take out an entire stand of red oaks while it left the bur oaks untouched."

As this is written, I'm still waiting for the lab analysis. That test will reveal only that oak wilt is, or is not, present in the tissue of the sample. If oak wilt is not present, the April 5 hard freeze is the most logical explanation.

Meanwhile, remember the rules about trimming and pruning oaks — leave them alone from April to July, the period when oaks are most susceptible to infection from fungus-carrying insects.

My advice: Don't plant Colorado blue spruce

When my wife and I built a home five years ago, one of the first landscaping decisions I made was to plant six Colorado blue spruce trees in the front yard. They've become nice-looking trees and are now over 10 feet tall. However, I wish I had never planted them.

Trees should be planted with a vision of how they will look 15 or 20 years from now. The problem with Colorado blue spruce is that they are vulnerable to a whole host of problems and will eventually begin to slide downhill (so to speak) due to environmental stress, insect damage and disease.

Colorado blue spruce have problems in this part of Minnesota because they are not native to the humid environment we experience in spring and summer. They prefer the more arid climate of the western mountain states.

I know criticizing this beloved evergreen species is a little like denigrating apple pie or the American flag. More Colorado blue spruce get planted in our landscapes, it seems, than any other tree. It's also the tree species that generates a large number of problem phone calls.

The most serious problem of Colorado blue spruce is dieback that starts near the bottom and center of the tree and works its way up until eventually the entire tree becomes disfigured. This condition is most often caused by Cytospora canker, a fungal disease that spreads during wet weather. Mike Zins, University of Minnesota extension horticulturist, refers to these disfigured trees as "Minnesota palm trees," because many people prune away the lower dead branches and leave the surviving green, healthy branches at the top.

Another common blue spruce fungal disease is Rhizosphaera

needle cast, which can cause a tree to shed its needles on the inner portions of the lower branches.

If you were to look closely at my six vigorous blue spruce, you would see that Cytospora canker, and maybe some Rhizosphaera needle cast, have begun to infect the lower branches. These diseases will most likely worsen in the years ahead. Carefully timed applications of a fungicide this time of year can prevent Rhizosphaera needle cast from infecting new growth. Chemical control is not an alternative, unfortunately, for Cytospora canker.

"Colorado blue spruce look so cute in the nursery — especially the blue forms when they're young — that many people can't resist planting them," explains Zins. "We need to get the word out that there are alternatives for people who like evergreens but want them to remain green and healthy for more than 10 or 15 years."

Here are some evergreen alternatives that Zins recommends (comments in quotes are from Manual of Woody Landscape Plants by Michael A. Dirr):

White Fir *(Abies concolor)* — White fir like warm, dry and sunny growing conditions. "Because of its growth habit and softer effect, it could well replace the spruces in the landscape; beautiful foliage, especially those trees with bluish needles."

Serbian Spruce *(Picea omorika)* — Can grow to 100 feet; "…a tree with a remarkably slender trunk and short ascending or drooping branches forming a very narrow, pyramidal head; one of the most graceful and beautiful spruces."

Norway Spruce *(Picea abies)* — Excellent resistance to disease but grows very large, so don't plant it where a very tall and wide evergreen tree would be a problem 25 years from now.

Black Hills Spruce *(Picea glauca densata)* — Somewhat more resistant to fungal diseases than Colorado blue spruce. Grows slowly to 40 feet tall.

Techny Arborvitae *(Thuja occidentalis)* — Also called white cedar. Severe winters can cause die-back and browning of arborvitaes, but Techny is one of the best-performing types. Grows to 15 feet. Of the cultivar 'Mission,' Dirr says "Excellent dark green foliage year-round, good hedge plant; probably the best form for northern gardens, extremely popular."

The longer I garden and the longer I answer questions from frustrated gardeners, the more I realize that no plant or garden is immune to disease and other problems.

My advice is to ask lots of questions about a tree or shrub before you buy it for your yard. What is its growth habit? How resistant is it to disease? What will it look like in 20 or 30 years?

When you purchase trees or shrubs, consider native species first, since they've survived in our local environment for centuries. Also look for disease-resistant and improved varieties.

And finally, "don't put all your eggs in one basket," horticulturally speaking. Don't plant your entire space to one species. Think rather in terms of a collection of plants. Create a "mini arboretum" in your yard. Then you won't feel so disheartened when one or two plants checks out for the great garden in the sky.

Tips for preventing winterkill on evergreens

Many people have called in recent weeks lamenting their dead-looking evergreens. Hardest hit seem to be yews and arborvitae, but spruce and pine also suffered significant winterkill.

Browning or bleaching of evergreen foliage occurs for three reasons:

1. Winter sun and wind cause excessive transpiration (foliage water loss) while the roots in frozen soil are unable to replace lost water. This results in desiccation and browning of the plant tissue.

2. Bright sunny days during the winter warm tissue above ambient temperature, which stimulates cellular activity. Then, at sunset, as foliage temperature drops suddenly to injurious levels, the tree can be injured or killed.

3. During bright, cold winter days, chlorophyll in the foliage is destroyed (photo oxidized) and is not resynthesized if the temperature is below 28 degrees. This results in bleaching of the foliage.

Winter browning occurs most often on the south, southwest and windward sides of the plant but, in severe cases, the whole plant may be affected.

If your evergreens suffered winter injury, there is no magic potion that will turn them green again. Best option is to prune out the injured foliage. The brown foliage is most likely dead and will not green up, but the buds, which are more cold hardy than the foliage, will often grow and fill in the area where the brown foliage was removed. If buds do not emerge, prune off the dead branches. Fertilize winter-injured plants now and water them weekly throughout the growing season (except during periods of excessive rainfall).

That's the bad news. The good news is that you can help evergreens prepare for next winter's severe conditions. The first way is to only plant evergreens bred for Zone 3 and 4 weather (Chaska is in Zone 4). Ask the retailer about the source of all plant material and don't plant anything that wasn't propagated in the north. Most reputable garden centers will tell you the origin of their plants.

Second, select a site that protects the evergreen from winter stress. Don't plant yew, arborvitae or hemlock on the south or southwest sides of buildings or in extremely windy or sunny areas.

Another technique is to protect evergreens from winter wind and sun by constructing a burlap barrier on the south and west sides. Or, you can stack pine boughs or some other homemade barrier to catch more snow for natural protection.

One person I talked to last week sounded borderline suicidal about her brown arborvitae. I asked her how long her arborvitae plants had been growing next to her house and she said about 18 years. I told her the best solution would be to cut them down and plant something new and fresh. Too often we think trees and shrubs should live forever. The fact is, there is always something new and exciting that we can select to replace a plant that has outlived its usefulness.

For gardeners, Saturday was a day to remember

I didn't write a column last week. I was too busy gardening. You probably didn't miss it for the same reason.

If weather came out of a catalog, you couldn't have ordered a better day for gardening and yard work than last Saturday. After months of enduring weird weather, Saturday was like a gift. My guess is that more Minnesota lawns were mowed Saturday than on any previous single day in the state's history.

For a gardener, the day was like being a kid in a candy store with a fistful of quarters. Where should I begin? How can I sample some of everything? Should I mow the lawn first, or pot annuals, or transplant tomatoes?

I decided to begin my day by transplanting petunias, which I had nurtured in my basement under florescent lights since March. I started two 1995 All-America Selections — Purple Wave and Celebrity Chiffon Morn. I haven't seen either variety in garden centers so I'm glad I went to the effort of ordering the seed and getting it started. I planted Purple Wave last year and was impressed with this cascading, prolific bloomer. This will be my first experience with Chiffon Morn, a "unique, soft pink with a delicate topping of cream and white in the center...that blends with most all garden colors."

As Saturday morning's stiff southwest breeze dried the grass, I got out the lawnmower and was pleased when it started. Unlike many conscientious gardeners, I did not winterize my Toro last fall so the sound of the engine was reassuring.

Later in the morning, a quick trip to town yielded a tray of annuals to fill in spaces among the perennials. I selected yellow marigolds to line the driveway in front of Stella d'Oro daylilies, and white alyssum for the front of another perennial bed.

I also replenished my supply of soil for container plants. Lots of folks ask about the best soil mixture for pots and containers. Expert gardeners often have a favorite mixture, but I have found that a variety of mixtures will get the job done.

This year I'm mixing bags of top soil and humus and adding compost from my compost bin. I probably should have mixed in some peat because it helps containers retain water. I use purchased pasteurized soil to minimize competition from weeds.

One of the great delights of spring is watching perennials emerge from the earth. Most of my hostas are in shady areas in ground covered with wood chips. This means that the soil warms very slowly and some of my hostas are only now making their appearance.

I also think some plants just plain refused to venture forth this crazy spring until they felt some serious heat. When the air temperature finally hit 80 degrees, they let out a shout and said it's time to "strut our stuff." In a matter of days, plants seemed to make up for lost time. I swear some of my hostas and other perennials (as well as the weeds!) grew an inch or more between walk-bys Saturday.

The same growth spurt was evident in the trees. Suddenly, trees we've been looking *through* for the past six months have formed a beautiful green curtain that blocks the more distant vista. From our picture window, May to October is like a telephoto view while the cold weather months provide a more panoramic view.

If farmers still followed the old adage of planting corn when oak leaves are the size of squirrels' ears, corn would just be going into the ground this week. Quite a few farmers had corn in the ground in late April this year. Of course, today's corn hybrids are bred to go in a lot earlier than the seed planted back when the old codger coined the "squirrels' ears" rule.

Good luck with your gardening adventures — try not to let the storms, weeds, insects, rabbits, deer and other obstacles get you down.

Bits and pieces about gardening in June...

A friend told me last week five dogwoods in his yard leafed out June 14! It's another indication of the severity of last winter.

My theory is that the record-setting cold drove some plants into such deep dormancy that it took the rains of early June followed by a week of hot days and warm nights to wake them up. It points to the need for restraint when the pruning urge strikes in May. Better to hold off a month or two until each plant reveals that it's truly done for.

Every June I get calls from people concerned about the strange bead-like growths on maple leaves. These are bladder galls caused by very small (1/170 inch) insects called eriophyid mites. Mites feed on the undersides of leaves which causes plant cells around the feeding site to become distorted. An individual bladder gall is about 1/16 to 1/8 inch diameter on the top surface of the leaf. While unsightly, the galls do not threaten the health of the tree. No treatment is recommended.

Every June I get calls from people concerned about the

By now you're likely well on your way to growing a 950 pound pumpkin and placing first in the Carver/Scott Master Gardener pumpkin growing contest. A word of warning — this is the time to watch closely for squash vine borer. Adult wasp-like moths are 1/2 inch long with an orange and black striped body. The first pair of wings is metallic green and the second pair is clear. Soon after emerging from their cocoons the moths lay eggs at the base of pumpkins and squash that hatch into caterpillars a week later. The young caterpillars bore into the stems and feed for 4 to 6 weeks. First sign of squash vine borer activity is a sudden wilting of plants. Close examination reveals an orange-green sawdust-like material oozing from the stem.

Resistant varieties deter squash vine borer, but if you notice a problem, dust the stems with carbaryl (Sevin) every week through the end of July.

❖

Did you know that dandelions were brought to this country by southern European immigrants who prized the leaves as pot herbs and salad greens? Dandelion flower heads open in the morning and close at night. Each yellow "petal" is a complete flower with a seed that develops at its base. Each dandelion flower contains 50 or more "petals" and seeds.

The best time to get rid of dandelions is September. If you kill most of them in autumn, they won't survive the winter to bloom next spring. Plants may sprout from seed, but they'll be small and easier to pull or treat than mature plants. Chemical of choice is 2,4-D. Read and follow label directions carefully.

Remember, too, that the best defense against dandelions is a thick, vigorous lawn, so fertilize, water and mow your lawn regularly.

❖

Speaking of weeds, one reason they're so hard to control is because they're so darn old. Many common weeds have survived for thousands of years. In fact, weeds are among the oldest living organisms and they didn't get that way by being stupid.

A Canadian botanist successfully propagated Arctic lupine from 10,000-year-old seeds that had been frozen in silt in Canada's Yukon Territory. A Michigan scientist mixed the seeds with sand in a milk bottle and buried the bottle, bottle mouth downward, in 1879. Some of the seeds sprouted when planted 100 years later.

My college horticulture professor said a weed is simply a flower out of place, so I guess it's just a matter of how you look at things.

Summer

Card-carrying Minnesotans should know a pine from a spruce

"This hole dog-legs to the right, so aim at that pine tree," my golfing partner advised.

There wasn't a pine in sight. Up ahead I saw a spruce, but certainly no pine.

"You mean that Colorado Blue Spruce 300 ahead yards ahead on the left side of the fairway?" I asked.

"Whatever," he said, not even pausing to acknowledge his faux pas. "That's right where you want to be for best approach to the green."

As golf advice, it was good. But how many other folks do you suppose this low-handicapper has steered the wrong direction, horticulturally speaking?

It's a funny thing about "evergreens" — most of us are enchanted by pine trees and spruce trees and other needle-bearing members of the conifer family, but when it comes to telling a pine from a spruce from a fir, many people don't have a clue.

Our enchantment with evergreens may stem from our association of evergreens with adventure or leisure vacation outings spent "up north." Our northern conifer forests are one of the main topographical differences between the northern and southern halves of Minnesota. Let's face it — listening to the wind whistle through the needles of a thick stand of Norway pine is a far more memorable sound than listening to wind blow through an elm tree.

I recall the half-day drive north my family took one week every August when I was a young farm boy visually accustomed to cow pastures and corn fields.

"It won't be long now," my dad used to say, somewhere in the vicinity of Little Falls or Long Prairie. "It won't be long now and we'll start seeing the 'tree line.'" He was referring to that area of our state where the oaks, maples and other hardwoods of central Minnesota give way to the dark green pyramidal shapes of millions of spruce and red and white pine.

I'd sit forward in the back seat of our '52 Buick and, for the next 50 miles or so, strain my eyes for the first sighting of that magical wall of pine and spruce.

Today, we've planted so many pine and spruce between here and Brainerd that the distinct treeline I remember from my youth no longer exists. In fact, depending on which road you travel, one might conclude that the tree line starts just north of Chaska and just keeps getting thicker as you drive north.

For the record, conifers are trees that don't drop their leaves (yes, needles are leaves) in the winter. Trees that drop their leaves each fall, like maples, ash and oaks, are called deciduous.

It is my belief that, as a card-carrying Minnesotan, you should — at the very least — be able to tell the difference between a pine and a spruce. Next time you're on a golf course, or walking outdoors anywhere else, for that matter, why not impress your friends with several of these distinctions between our most popular conifers.

Red (Norway) pine *(Pinus resinosa)* is Minnesota's state tree. It has 5- to 6-inch long stiff needles, two to a cluster, that snap or break clean when bent.

White pine *(Pinus strobus)* has 2- to 4-inch long needles, five to a cluster, that are soft, fine and flexible.

Scotch pine *(Pinus sylvestris)* has 2-inch long twisted needles, two to a cluster, and orangish-tan bark.

Blue spruce *(Picea pungens)* has very sharp 1-inch needles, borne singly, that are rectangular in cross section. Needles can be green, bluish-green or blue.

White spruce *(Picea glauca densata)* is commonly known as Black Hills spruce. Needles, which are borne singly, are slightly shorter than blue spruce needles and not as sharp.

Other conifers common to this area include northern white cedar, eastern red cedar, Norway spruce, Balsum fir, Douglas fir and eastern hemlock.

Now, if you want to really impress your friends, tell them about the eastern larch (tamarack). This is a decidious conifer

— it drops its needles in the winter and grows a new batch each spring.

By the way, I sliced my drive and took a double bogey on that hole. I should have aimed at that pine tree...

Midsummer musings on the joy and pain of gardening

Each gardening year is unique.

I will remember this spring and summer as the year I didn't even have to remove the spider webs from my lawn sprinklers. Daily rains — or at least rains every three or four days — have kept my lawn and flower beds adequately moist. It appears we may be entering a dryer period in the weeks ahead, so watering may once again become a routine part of gardening chores.

I'll also remember 1998 as the year of the chainsaw. I lost large trees or limb sections in three different storms. As a result, I now have sufficient firewood to last for a decade or more. Of course, much of it still needs to be split and dried.

If you're given a lemon, make lemonade. That's how I decided to view the giant red oak that crashed in my front yard. Its decay had begun years ago, much to the delight of a very large family of squirrels. As I approached the large hollow trunk section with my chainsaw, I began to see possibilities beyond firewood.

The base of the trunk split down the middle, leaving two 10-foot hollowed out slabs that resembled dugout canoes. Too big to move by hand, they will become horizontal planters next year right on the spot where they landed in the storm. Other 2-foot cross sections of the intact hollow trunk have already become planters for Gaillardia (blanket flower) I started from seed last winter.

One bright side to the spring storms is that many of the trees that toppled in our region were quite likely "hazard trees" prior to the storm. They had begun to decay and were destined to fall in a storm some time. The bright side is that the remaining trees in our rural and urban forest are probably quite healthy and strong and should be able to withstand strong winds in future storms better than the trees that went down.

Like so many gardeners I talk with, I have cursed the blight that slowly destroys tomato plants. This year, in an attempt to outsmart blight, I put my six tomato plants in large pots and am growing them near the front door of my house. Every day, as I carry letters to the mailbox or pick up the mail, I fill the containers with water from the hose. Growing tomatoes in pots requires a lot of water but if water and nutrients are added regularly, tomatoes can perform very well in pots. To this point, I haven't had problems with blight.

One of the delightful aspects of growing perennial flowers is watching them spread from year to year through root action or reseeding. Several years ago I started a half dozen Rudbeckia fulgida (black-eyed Susan) from seed. The plants have multiplied from the seeds I've scattered in the fall, and I now have scores of blooming plants that provide wonderful eye appeal.

I was enthused early in the season about the bountiful crop of tiny apples that had emerged on my young Haral Red apple tree. Then a wind storm tore off a major limb holding about 30 apples and I was forced to reluctantly carry away the apple-laden branch. Now the increasing weight of the remaining apples is causing other limb sections to sag precariously. I've tied several of the branches up with support ties and have my fingers crossed that the windstorms are over. My early excitement about a large apple crop has been replaced by concern for the tree's capability to nurture the apples to maturity.

A discussion of this gardening season wouldn't be complete without mentioning the bumper crop of mosquitoes that appeared in early July. In my shady backyard, I can stand about 30 seconds of watering hanging pots before a hoard of pesky skeeters sends me fleeing to the sunny front yard. The other day, I made the mistake of wearing shorts while watering and my legs looked like that old television commercial where the man sticks his arms into a glass chamber of mosquitoes to demonstrate a leading bug repellent. (My legs resembled the arm that wasn't sprayed.)

I don't mind summer heat. But combine heat with a cloud of mosquitoes and some of the joy of gardening disappears. Wear lots of clothes and a head net and the heat becomes suffocating. Spray the body with bug repellent and soon the chemical is in the eyes and a shower is mandatory the second you step indoors.

I hope there are no mosquitoes in your yard and that your joys are outnumbering your pains as you tend your garden this summer.

Hybrid poplars attracting attention of state's land owners

Imagine trees that grow from rootstock to 20 feet or more by the second year!

A show plot of hybrid poplars at this summer's Farmfest near Redwood Falls drew heavy interest from a variety of visitors:

- Farmers and investors researching a new cash crop;
- Home owners interested in a quick-growing windbreak;
- Land owners searching for a way to cash-crop their CRP acres;
- Curiosity seekers wondering how a tree can grow so fast.

Along with solar energy and windmills, hybrid poplars got a boost in the late 1970s during the oil embargo. University of Minnesota and state foresters began evaluating thousands of crosses of the genus *Populus* (aspen, cottonwood, poplar) for their energy producing potential and other characteristics.

According to Steve Von Groven, a DNR forester at Mora, researchers have identified eight very promising hybrids that are resistant to both insects and disease and grow fast. These hybrids mature in 8-15 years and yield 3-5 cords/acre/year.

The Farmfest demonstration plot has first-year trees that stand about 3 feet tall and a second-year stand that towers to 20 feet. These trees are spaced 4 feet apart and will be thinned to 8 feet next year. The stand is so thick it is difficult to walk between the trees.

If you've ever had difficulty counting annual rings of a felled tree, you'd marvel at the rings of hybrid poplar. On a 10-year-old cross section I examined, the rings were more than a half inch thick; a 10-year-old tree, therefore, exceeds 10 inches in diameter!

Hybrid poplars are being encouraged as an agricultural crop in part because Minnesota's supply of aspen is inadequate to support our state's expanding paper manufacturing industry.

At present prices, hybrid poplar won't produce a return equal to corn or soybeans. After 10 years of growth, a plantation of hybrid poplar should yield 40 cords/acre and have a value of $1,200. Cost to establish an acre of hybrid poplar is approximately $300, and some maintenance costs will be incurred during the first couple of years for weed control (by the third year, trees shade out weeds).

One possible scenario that may be economically viable is to plant hybrid poplars on CRP (Conservation Reserve Program) acres and harvest the crop at the end of 10 years when the CRP contract is over.

Skeptics of hybrid poplars include land owners who planted windbreaks of fast-growing Lombardy poplars 20 or 30 years ago and then watched them die prematurely from canker disease that starts in the upper branches and works its way down. The hybrid poplars available from Lee Nursery in Fertile, Minnesota and Schumacher Nursery in Heron Lake, Minnesota, are not susceptible to canker disease, according to Von Groven. He recommends ordering cuttings of at least three different clones to spread the risk of possible disease or insect infestations.

Interest in hybrid poplars for windbreaks is widespread in rural Minnesota because so many windbreaks were destroyed last December when the ice storm tore apart ash and other grove trees. While poplars drop their leaves like other deciduous trees, they provide enough of a wind barrier to trap snow at the perimeter of a building site. For windbreaks, Von Groven suggests planting three rows of poplars spaced 8 feet apart — closer if you are willing to thin them later.

Hybrid poplars will not perform in extremely wet or dry soils, or where soil pH exceeds 7.5, Von Groven says.

I don't recommend hybrid poplars for the average urban lot where you're looking for shade or a stately specimen tree. For these purposes, plant a red or swamp white oak, sugar or red maple, river birch or linden.

But if you are searching for a fast-growing windbreak...or if you want to reap a return on your investment in trees 10 years from now...or if you want to create heavy cover for birds and wildlife...then hybrid poplars may be a good choice.

Sightseeing bike ride ends up in blueberry patch

One thing always seems to lead to another. A sightseeing bike ride Saturday led me to the fields of Carver Nursery on Mt. Carmel road southwest of Carver. Riding down a field path, I applied my brakes as a customer popped a plump red raspberry into his mouth. Fresh raspberries — what a refreshing reward for the 10 miles I had just pedaled!

I circled around to Carver Nursery's office area and found owner Jim Freeman collecting wrenches for a machine maintenance project. "I've got a real treat for you," he offered. "The blueberries are ripe."

Freeman led me through the maze of nursery trees to several long rows of low-growing blueberry bushes, their branches bending under the weight of succulent blue fruit. A family was busy filling flats with berries destined, I overheard, for jam and muffins. Behind me in a stand of red pines, a robin eyed the action hungrily.

I made two decisions fairly quickly. First, I knew I'd have to pick some berries for my own kitchen. And second, transporting blueberries home on a bicycle was not a smart idea.

The Hwy. 43 hill didn't seem quite as steep as I pondered the return trip by car and breakfast cereal in the days ahead topped with a layer of fresh raspberries and blueberries. When I returned, Freeman unwrapped the plastic netting that protects his blueberry bushes from hungry birds. Without the netting, Freeman said, the birds would strip the bushes of berries in less than a day.

The best way to pick blueberries is to wait until most of the fruit is fully ripe. At this stage, a handful of ripe berries can be "raked" off the stem into a waiting pine box — a much faster process than picking berries individually.

I filled two boxes with blueberries, then moved to the long rows of juicy raspberries and filled four more boxes. Along the way, one or two raspberries found their way into my mouth.

Growing blueberries here in central Minnesota isn't as easy as growing many other fruit species because blueberries require acidic soils not common in most local landscapes. I have two blueberry plants that were attacked by rabbits the first winter following planting. I've since surrounded the plants with wire cages to keep out critters but the yellow leaves indicate a nutrient deficiency that needs correcting.

Blueberry plants grow best in soils with a pH of 4.0 to 5.0 (our average soil pH in Carver and Scott counties is much higher). Soils not within the range of pH acceptability for blueberry plant growth must be prepared before planting. If your soil contains a lot of clay or heavy loam, you will have to replace this soil with a sand and peat mixture. The University recommends removing unsuitable soils from a space 15 in. deep by at least 2 ft. wide.

The most satisfactory results will be obtained by digging an entire bed, rather than digging holes for individual plants. For just a few plants, consider growing blueberries in pots containing the appropriate soil mixture. Even with proper bed preparation, supplemental sulfur compounds will most likely be needed to maintain the acidic soils conditions necessary for fruit production.

The University of Minnesota fruit breeding program has released blueberry varieties suitable for our climate. More than one of the following should be planted to achieve optimum pollination: North Blue, North Country, North Sky and St. Cloud.

If you've read this far, you've probably concluded that growing blueberries is fairly complicated. If you want to give it a try, I suggest you do some additional research before bringing home plants from the garden center. An even better idea would be to grow something else in your garden, and simply stop by Carver Nursery each July and August to pick your own!

Help Arboretum celebrate its 40th birthday this summer

Last Thursday, I had my first guided tour of the Minnesota Landscape Arboretum (MLA). Although I've visited the MLA hundreds of times, I never rode the special tram or listened to a tour guide's description of the MLA's dozens of beautiful gardens and plant collections.

Our guide was Peter Moe, the MLA's director of operations. As we left the Snyder Building and passed by the many specialty gardens, I thought about how we so often go to showrooms to pick out our cars, kitchens and bathrooms. Why don't more homeowners go to the many "showrooms" at the Arboretum to pick out their front yards, backyards, hedges and flower gardens? It makes perfect sense to me, especially with the building boom taking place in many parts of Scott and Carver County.

This is the 40th anniversary of the MLA and Moe and his staff have the grounds in beautiful condition. Admission is even free on Thursday evenings! If you're contemplating any changes in your home gardens, I highly recommend a stop at one or more of these MLA display gardens:

Home Demonstration Gardens — There are nine individual gardens at this site, and each is designed to inspire ideas that you can apply at home. There's a rock garden, a container garden, a garden for small spaces, an herb garden, a cut-flower garden, a garden for outdoor living, a small fruit and vegetable garden, a naturalized garden, a deck and patio garden, and an open planting area that is planted each year to different and unusual plants.

Wilson Rose Garden — If roses are your passion, this colorful space features more than 200 varieties of hybrid teas, floribundas and grandifloras. One of the most beautiful weddings I've attended took place in this garden, which offers wheel-chair access. Dozens more old-fashioned and shrub roses are displayed further out on the Arboretum's 3-mile drive.

Howard Fern and Hosta Glade — Walk along shady paths and view many varieties of ferns and more than 300 varieties of hostas — one of the largest hosta displays in the U.S.

Culinary Herb Garden — Herbs are attracting much more attention these days, and this garden features dozens of plants that can be used for cooking, including basil, thyme, sage, garlic and many exotic herbs.

Wildflower Garden — Wildflowers are capturing the imagination of more and more gardeners, and this newly renovated area promises to be spectacular in the years ahead. Bring along a notebook when you visit this area because you'll want to jot down the names of some of these beautiful but unfamiliar plants.

Bennett/Johnson Prairie — When the glaciers receded 10,000 years ago, nearly one-third of Minnesota was covered by a sea of grass and flowering plants known as tallgrass prairie. The Bennett/Johnson Prairie is a broad collection of native species found within the prairie communities of the Upper Midwest. If you've thought about establishing native prairie on your property, I highly recommend a visit to this beautiful wild area. A blooming prairie tour takes place every Sunday at 1 p.m.

Weeping and Small Tree Collections — If you're searching for just the right small or unusual tree for your yard, a visit to this section of the MLA's 3-mile drive can give you some great ideas. Specimens include pea shrubs, willows, crab apples, blue beech, smoke bush, fringe tree, apricot, hawthorn, Peking lilac, and many varieties of evergreens.

Hedge Collection —Hedges in this display have been created from a surprisingly diverse range of trees and shrubs. I won't even begin to name them all, but if establishing a hedge is on your to-do list, visit this area for some great ideas.

Ornamental Grasses — Dr. Mary Meyer, director of the state Master Gardener program, has been conducting some very useful research in recent years on which ornamental grasses perform best in our harsh Minnesota climate. If you want to add year-round visual interest to your landscape, take a look at these grasses during August or September and note the grass you like best. Some of the best grasses for our area are in the Miscanthus family and grow to 9 ft. tall!

Shade Trees — My specialty as a Master Gardener is trees and I answer hundreds of phone calls from homeowners each year about tree problems resulting from insects, disease and the environment. Many problems faced by tree owners can be prevented by proper tree selection.

One of the best ways to ensure that you select the right tree is to observe many varieties of trees growing at various stages of maturity. The best place I know to observe trees is the MLA. I've described just a handful of the MLA's beautiful gardens and displays. I hope you will visit the MLA soon, and don't forget to pack a camera and notebook.

Beautiful, easy-care shrub roses goal of local project

Kathy Zuzek is in charge of rose breeding at the University's horticulture research center on Highway 5. Several weeks ago, she led a group through the shrub rose breeding and evaluation project she coordinates at the center.

The center's shrub rose project got a boost several years ago when it inherited a collection of 87 shrub rose cultivars developed by Dr. Griffith Buck (now deceased) at Iowa State University in the 1970s and '80s.

The goal of Zuzek's work is to develop shrub roses that will perform in USDA Zone 4 (northern Iowa to central Minnesota). To "make the cut" in Zuzek's breeding and selection process, shrub roses have to exhibit six primary traits:

1. Winter hardiness without special winter protection.
2. Resistance to black spot, powdery mildew and other common rose diseases.
3. Insect resistance.
4. Capacity to flower prolifically.
5. Capacity to rebloom through the growing season.
6. Proper plant size and growth habit.

Zuzek demonstrated the process of pollinating shrub roses. First she peels all the petals off a flower, then removes the anthers. Pollen from another rose is applied to the stigmas and then aluminum foil is wrapped around the remaining flower part to keep out unwanted pollen. Each cross is carefully labeled. If the pollination is successful, the fruit grows and produces a rose "hip" containing 30-40 seeds.

These seeds are collected and stratified (chilled) for 60-90 days, then sown to germinate in February. Young seedlings are grown in pots for one year, then transplanted in the ground at the research center for further evaluation.

Some of the experimental shrub roses bloom in their first year, Zuzek said, while others may not bloom until the third year.

Shrub roses in the project are evaluated every two weeks during the growing season to see how well they exhibit the six traits mentioned above.

Some roses in the program are propagated from softwood stem cuttings. After a stem is cut, it is dipped in a rooting hormone and planted in a moist mixture of nine parts perlite and one part peat. Zuzek led us inside the greenhouse housing these cuttings. Instantly, our glasses steamed up — the environment must be kept at 100% humidity. Zuzek said that, even on a hot day, stepping out of this greenhouse feels like stepping into an air-conditioned room!

Let's hope Zuzek's efforts are successful because the result will be attractive new shrub rose cultivars for our gardens that require only a fraction of the labor and attention than many other types of roses.

By the way, Zuzek said her program is always "understaffed" and in need of volunteers to help with hybridizing, sorting seeds and evaluating and recording performance data. If you are interested in helping out, call her at 474-6886.

For dazzling flowers, begin with All-America selections

Ever wonder why some gardener's flowers look like a cover photo from *Better Homes & Gardens* while yours may not quite achieve the picture you had in mind at planting time?

Sure, some gardeners just have that proverbial "green thumb" and could grow daisies in the dark. One secret of the pros that you can take advantage of, however, is to select better varieties of flowers to begin with.

Each year, the National Garden Bureau designates several varieties of annuals and perennials as All-American Selections. Flowers that receive AAS status have been tested and proven to be vigorous and floriferous — many are downright spectacular in their capacity to send forth bountiful, beautiful and long-lasting blooms.

The good news is that you can grow these AAS flowers in your garden simply by ordering and starting seed prior to the growing season, or by buying these plants in spring from reputable garden centers.

There are many AAS flowers I haven't planted — they're still on my "wish" and "to-do" lists. Several that I have planted, and highly recommend to you, include:

'Purple Wave' Petunias — The name says it all...Purple Wave petunias send out wave after wave of brilliant purple blossoms from spring to late summer. I started Purple Wave petunias from seed in my basement in March and planted only four plants in a large half-barrel wooden tub. They quickly filled the container and sent dozens of runners over the sides. I've had a mass of purple blossoms up until last week, when I cut them back because they were starting to look a little spent. Now a whole new growth of foliage has started and I'll have more waves of purple right up to frost.

Many petunias bloom nicely for a couple of weeks and then get leggy and somewhat unsightly. Not so with Purple Wave — they just keep on blooming and sending out more blossoms on more runners. Burpee Seeds, my source for the seed, describes Purple Wave petunias as "the first-ever ground cover petunia. This 'magic carpet' of deep burgundy purple never gets over 4 inches tall. One plant will cover 3-4 feet of bed or fill a basket."

Purple Wave petunias are at their show-off best in window boxes, planters and hanging baskets.

Gloriosa Daisy 'Indian Summer' — This spectacular yellow daisy begins sporting its large 3-inch yellow flowers in July and keeps sending up more blossoms right up to frost. Like the petunias, I started them from seed in March and they bloomed prolifically the first year. A member of the Rudbeckia family, this black-eyed Susan-type flower should behave like a perennial and reappear next spring.

Coreopsis 'Moonbeam' — The 1992 Perennial Plant of the Year, this classy 14-inch plant sends forth hundreds of creamy-yellow flowers on thread-leaf foliage. This plant blooms right up to frost and is a terrific choice for the front of borders. My "moonbeams" started out in a clayey soil that was too wet and did poorly. Last summer I moved them to a drier spot and ever since they've been just as happy as robins after rain.

Sedum 'Autumn Joy' — Although not an AAS to my knowledge, this member of the stone crop family has been called "...arguably the best perennial that can be planted in Minnesota." Large, flat clusters of pink flowers emerge in late summer, then turn coppery red in fall atop mounds of silver-green fleshy foliage. Sturdy plants bloom right up to frost, then turn an attractive rust color and stand erect all winter above the snow. I don't cut off the stems until new growth begins appearing early in the spring — it's a showy 12-month Minnesota perennial.

Soil that moves? You needed to be there...

Some of the strangest things happen in gardening. I had an astilbe seedling in a 4-inch pot, which I intended to transplant after it got bigger. The pot was in a tray of young plants that I walked by often.

During several walkbys last week, it seemed like the soil in that pot moved as I passed but I didn't stop to examine the situation more closely. Soil is inert; it doesn't move, right?

Next trip by, the soil moved again. This is too weird, I thought, and I set down my pails to take a closer look. Sure enough, the soil was moving. The reason? A toad had taken up residence in the center of the pot and scrunched down low each time I walked by.

The toad had uprooted the astilbe plant to make a comfortable lair in the cool, moist peat. I didn't get too upset over the loss of the astilbe. I mean, how many gardeners have mastered the art of growing toads in pots?

❖

For all the sprinkles and clouds lately, it's easy to assume the ground is saturated. The fact is, the ground is bone dry, especially around trees that are drawing up hundreds of gallons of water to produce leaves, flowers, fruit and nuts. I'm trying to establish a perennial garden under a basswood tree and the soil surface resembles a desert.

If you have young trees, shrubs or perennials that aren't fully established, don't forget to give them a healthy drink at least once a week. It's been a peculiar year for weather. The High Plains and Texas Panhandle are experiencing a drought that rivals the dust bowl days. In between, in Missouri and Iowa, rains have delayed planting and flooded rivers and streams.

And here in the north country, the rains seem to pass just to our north or south.

❖

It's time to keep a close watch for sawfly larvae feeding on new growth of spruce and pine. Sawfly larvae are just under 1 inch in length and have a black head and yellow-green striped body. They feed in groups and can defoliate a spruce or pine in days.

The key to control is to stop defoliation before it becomes too extensive. Insecticides that control sawfly larvae include malathion, carbaryl (Sevin) and acephate (Orthene). These chemicals are mixed with water and sprayed on the tree. If you notice an infestation and attempt to spray your trees yourself, follow mixing and application directions carefully.

❖

If you've been gardening this spring, perhaps you've become aware of how good you feel. An article on healing in the June/July Minnesota Horticulturist states that, when people get in touch with nature, their heart rate slows, their muscles loosen and the blood pressure drops. Even the way skin conducts electricity suggests a positive emotional state, the article reports.

The Minnesota Landscape Arboretum just up the road in Chanhassen completed in 1995 its Clotilde Irvine Sensory Garden. The garden "serves as a regional resource for professional therapists, disabled individuals, and representatives from nursing homes." All surfaces are wheelchair accessible. Check it out.

❖

Pumpkin Update: Some night creature (a raccoon? a wood chuck?) dug up one of my precious giant pumpkin plants and left a 10-inch hole. My four other plants are just beginning to vine. Hard to believe one of these plants will give birth to a 750-pound trophy pumpkin in just a couple of months! How are your pumpkins doing?

If your yard must have a birch tree, plant a river birch

Rarely a week goes by that doesn't include two or three phone calls from people worried about their birch trees. If you think of the trees in your yard as your kids, birch are the "problem children." Why all the problems?

Each summer, thousands of folks from here in southern Minnesota travel "Up North" and are captivated by the striking white bark and glistening leaves of birch. "If only we had one of those in our front yard," they reason, "life would be peachy." So they dig a clump out of the shady, cool, damp forest and plunk it down smack in the middle of their sunny, dry front yard. And guess what? The tree doesn't do so well. The reason is simple: Birch prefer cool, moist sites. That's why so many of them grow in the cool, moist, boggy northern forest. I've hiked many miles in the Boundary Waters Canoe Area and it's not uncommon to sink ankle-deep in the wet soil and moss found at the base of paper birch.

I agree that a clump of birch does look nice in a front yard. The thing to remember, though, is that a sunny front yard is not their first-choice for growing sites and they may show their displeasure by growing in that spot for a relatively short time span — say 10 to 15 years.

Birch trees planted in landscapes where conditions are different from their native habitat suffer stress. And stressed birch trees succumb to two serious insect pests — the bronze birch borer and birch leaf miners. Bronze birch borers can kill a stressed birch tree within a few years of planting.

If you have your heart set on a birch, there are some things you can do to improve your chances of growing a healthy tree.

Birch trees should be fertilized in the spring, watered

throughout the summer, and mulched with an organic mulch to keep the soil cool beneath the trees. Keeping birches in good condition minimizes birch borer problems.

The most common species of birch planted in Minnesota are white (paper) birch *(Betula papyrifera)*, European birch *(Betula pendula)*, and river birch *(Betula nigra)*. Of the three, river birch is the best bet for a front or back yard. True, it doesn't have the white paper bark that people like so much, but its bark is unique — it, too, is loose and papery, with a reddish-brown coloring that darkens as the tree becomes older.

River birch are much more resistant to the bronze birch borer than either European or paper birch. All the birch can be planted as a single stem or as a clump tree.

Two other birch species that are more resistant to bronze birch borers than the white-barked birches are sweet birch *(Betula lenta)* and yellow birch *(Betula alleghaniensis)*. Sweet birch can grow to 50 feet and has outstanding yellow fall color. Its bark is smooth and dark reddish-brown. Yellow birch can grow to 75 feet and also have terrific yellow fall color. Oil of wintergreen can be extracted from the stem and bark of sweet and yellow birch.

Here's the bottom line: If you have your heart set on a birch tree, plant a river birch with 3 to 5 stems. Select a planting site in the coolest, moistest area of your yard, give the tree plenty of water and mulch, and avoid compacting the soil surrounding the tree. Good luck!

Groundcovers good alternative to grass in special sites

"Ground cover" is a term used to describe a wide range of plants — more than 300 species — that are used to form a thick "cover" in a particular space. Their height can range from 1 inch to 4 feet.

Gardeners choose ground covers for a variety of reasons:

- Unify unrelated landscape elements;
- Provide an attractive alternative to grass in shady areas;
- Define or emphasize certain areas or features;
- "Soften" harsh walls and embankments;
- Control soil erosion on slopes.

The most widely used ground cover, of course, is turf grass. Gardeners often choose grass because of its dense, uniform growth and ability to withstand foot traffic.

I've been experimenting with ground covers because I think they're more interesting than turf grass and because the dense shade in much of my yard isn't suitable for growing grass.

On the surface, the idea seems idyllic — an attractive plant that forms a thick canopy, chokes out weeds and never needs mowing. Be aware, however, that the number of plants needed to cover a large area can cost considerably more than turf grass and may take 3-4 years to fill in like the pretty photos in the mail order catalog. The most economical way to convert an area to a ground cover is to thin out — with permission! — a friend or neighbor's established stand.

Here are some of the ground covers I'm using and some thoughts about each.

Pachysandra (*Pachysandra terminalis*) — Also known as Japanese Spurge. Grows to about 1 foot tall and spreads by underground stems to form a dense mat with glossy yellow-green leaves. Likes partial to heavy shade and performs well under trees. When planted 8 inches apart, pachysandra will take about 3 years to fill in completely. The best price I've seen is 1,000 plants for $290 from Musser Forests, a mail order nursery in Pennsylvania.

Myrtle *(Vinca minor)* — Also known as common periwinkle. I planted about 200 bare-root clumps of 10 runners each and only about half the clumps survived last winter. Once established, myrtle forms an attractive 6-inch mat of trailing stems and leaves. Suitable for partial sun or shade. Myrtle has funnel-shaped lilac-blue flowers in spring.

Bugleweed *(Ajuga reptans)* — Forms a dense mat 4-6 inches high with violet-blue flowers in May. Many cultivars are available; the most common have purple-bronze colored leaves. It spreads quickly by stolens that root at the nodes and will grow in full sun to heavy shade. Like myrtle, bugleweed is subject to winterkill if not protected by snowcover or a cover of mulch.

Creeping Charlie *(Glechoma hederacea)* — Now don't laugh — this vigorous ground-hugger is hardy, spreads fast and has pretty lavender/purple flowers in April and May. Plant it in an area where grass won't grow. Some cultivars are less invasive than "the weed" and sport attractive leaves.

Creeping Jenny *(Lysimachia nummularia)* — Also known as moneywort. It's not as invasive as Creeping Charlie, sending out 2-foot ground-hugging stems that are dotted with yellow flowers in June — an attractive groundcover for shade.

Barrenwort *(Epimedium* species) — I planted one clump to see how it would perform and am hopeful that a much thicker clump will emerge next spring. The Arboretum has several healthy stands on the patio behind the Snyder Building. Many regard epimedium as the best all-around groundcover. It grows about 1-foot high; some cultivars spread vigorously by underground rhizomes. Plant in partial to heavy shade.

Hostas — Hostas are probably my favorite ground cover. The only reason I don't have more is their higher relative cost. Hostas love shade and are available in an almost limitless range of leaf shapes and colorations. Mix them to create bold, distinctive landscape effects. The flowers of hostas, borne in summer, are secondary to their showy leaves.

This listing only scratches the surface of what's available in the world of ground covers. One book in my library, "Ground-covers for the Midwest," lists more than 300 woody and herbaceous plants that behave as ground covers.

If you're interested in converting part of your yard to ground covers, I recommend taking a notebook and pencil to the Arboretum and record names of ground covers you like. Then locate a gardener with that species and comment that their stand looks awfully thick. Hopefully they'll respond, "Yeah, it really needs to be thinned out, but I've been so busy." That's when you reach for your shovel.

Don't let construction damage do in your precious trees

About the quickest way to kill a tree, short of cutting it down, is to build something next to it.

I get a lot of calls from folks asking what might be wrong with their tree because it's dropping leaves, or half of it appears to be dying. A few perfunctory questions generally reveal that, yes, they did dig a foundation 4 feet away last year, or, yes, they cut some roots off to put in the swimming pool.

I've driven through housing developments that have been carved out of wooded areas. Two or three years after completion, it's very common (and depressing) to see mature oaks or maples wilting and dropping their leaves. Too often, the root systems of these trees were damaged during home, street or utility construction.

Construction damage can take a variety of forms: Severed roots from digging basements, footings, utility trenches or sewage systems; root compaction by heavy equipment; torn bark; trunk or branch injuries; and poisoning from toxic spills.

Most large trees near proposed construction sites are worth saving. Some tree species are more sensitive to construction damage than others. Among the most sensitive to root severance are white oaks, northern pin oaks and black walnut. Trees that are sensitive to root compaction include pine, birch, basswood, maple, red oak and white oak.

Prior to the arrival of construction equipment, there are some common-sense precautions that can maximize your chances of preserving your trees' overall good health.

First of all, consider that up to 95% of a tree's root system can be in the top 3 feet of soil, and more than half of a tree's roots are in the top 1 foot of soil. Professional arborists define the part of the root zone in which construction damage should be avoided as the "Protected Root Zone" (PRZ).

Historically, a common rule of thumb has been to avoid disturbing roots inside of the "dripline" — the area directly below the branches of the tree. However, since roots can extend horizontally up to two or more times the height of the tree, a safer guideline is to protect an area equivalent to 18 inches for each 1 inch of trunk diameter (e.g., for a 2-foot diameter tree, protect the area within 36 feet of the trunk).

I don't think it's a worthy goal to protect every tree around a building site. Cottonwoods, box elders, silver maples, spruce, elm and willow probably aren't worth saving, for a variety of reasons. It's better to remove these trees before construction and plant more desirable trees once construction is complete.

The best way to protect trees during construction is to agree with the builder and architect ahead of time on what trees are "off limits," and then install bright orange polypropylene fencing around the PRZ. Make sure your contractor and all subcontractors understand that nothing between the tree trunk and the fence is to be raked, dug, cut, driven on or dumped on.

My house near Chaska was built by Dave Durst in 1993 amidst mature bur oaks and basswoods. All the trees are still healthy today because Dave understood their value and instructed each subcontractor to follow the above rules.

Even if you want to save a tree closer than the PRZ — say 10-15 feet from the building site — there are some tricks you can use to increase the chances of a tree's survival; for details, drop me a note and we can discuss it further.

It's not always easy to save trees during construction but your efforts are worth the trouble. Healthy, well-placed trees can increase property values by up to 25%.

If you are planning a construction project, the best first-step is to consult with an urban forester or arborist with experience in protecting trees from construction damage. Check the yellow pages under "Tree Service."

Formula for butterflies: Nectar plants, habitat, no pesticides

Julie, a fellow Master Gardener, counted 11 species of butterflies in her garden last summer and she's optimistic she will
exceed that total this year because of new knowledge and pol-
ished techniques.

Each of us can attract butterflies to our yards by selecting
desirable nectar plants and by following a handful of other butterfly attracting rules.

Near the top of Julie's list of rules is to refrain from using
pesticides. To attract butterflies, we must also protect the caterpillars that become butterflies. Consider this: A spectacular 5-
inch tiger swallowtail butterfly starts out as a 2-1/2-inch green
caterpillar that eats leaves of ash, cherry, willow and birch trees.

How many of us, when we come face to face with a 2-1/2-
inch green caterpillar, respond with horror and reach for a can
of Raid? That kind of response is not compatible, Julie says,
with creating an ideal environment for butterflies.

The three primary rules for attracting butterflies are to plant
the right plants, offer an attractive habitat, and avoid pesticides.

The goal in plant selection is to provide flowers in bloom
throughout the season. Many annuals are wonderful butterfly
plants because they bloom continuously and provide a steady
supply of nectar. Perennials such as coneflowers, lilacs, butterfly weed and asters are visited regularly by butterflies, and
most plants in the mint family are also good nectar sources.
Plants with double flowers are often bred for showiness and do
not produce plentiful nectar.

Julie's two favorite plants are butterfly bush (Buddleia) and
Verbena bonariensis.

Some of the best food sources for butterfly caterpillars may be the vegetables growing in your garden. Black swallowtail butterfly caterpillars, for example, like to feed on parsley, carrot, dill and parsnip. Sulphur butterfly caterpillars search out clover, alfalfa and false indigo. The caterpillar of the silver-spotted great spangled butterfly feeds on violets. And you'll most likely discover the caterpillar of the painted lady butterfly feeding on thistles — perhaps the only reason not to rid your yard of this weed pest.

Several habitat considerations for attracting butterflies include providing shelter from wind and a "puddling area." Butterflies prefer to feed and lay eggs in sunny, sheltered areas. Windbreaks can be created with shrubs and trees. Butterflies will congregate at the edge of mud puddles or wet sandy areas where they imbibe fluids rich in salts and nutrients.

Pesticides and butterflies definitely don't mix. Instead of using broad-spectrum chemicals on your lawn and plants, consider alternative control methods such as oils, soaps and microbial insecticides such as Bacillus thuringiensis (Bt). Even oils and insecticidal soaps can kill caterpillars if sprayed directly on the insect. Caterpillars will also die if they feed on plants treated with a Bt formulation that is toxic to them.

Most butterfly species, such as the tiger swallowtail, lay only a few eggs at a time. This low level of insect population will not kill shrubs or trees, advises Vera Krischik, a University of Minnesota entomologist and butterfly expert. One exception, she says, is the black swallowtail larvae, which can completely defoliate a dill plant.

When you discover a worm or caterpillar feeding on your plants, take a little extra time to identify the critter — it may be just days away of becoming a beautiful, soaring butterfly.

The "do's and don'ts" I've outlined here suggest that any desire to attract butterflies should be followed up with some careful research. There are many wonderful references on butterflies available at bookstores and garden centers. A good place to start is the bookstore at the Minnesota Landscape Arboretum.

Here are some suggested nectar plants for adult butterflies.

Shrubs — Azaleas, blueberries, butterfly bush, button bush, lilac, privet, sumac.

Annuals — Impatiens, nicotiana, coneflowers, marigold, phlox, sunflower, verbena.

Perennials — Asters, butterfly weed, chrysanthemums, daisies, monarda, purple coneflower, sedum, yarrow.

Wildflowers — New England aster, black-eyed Susan, blazing star, Joe-Pye weed, coreopsis, dogbane, goldenrod, ironweed, milkweed, monarda, ox-eye.

Monsoon season offers new array of gardening challenges

The view from my window today is reminiscent of a rain forest. The relentless downpour signals that my rain gauge needs emptying — just under three inches of rain have fallen since midnight; 11-3/4 inches since June 28.

Less than a month ago I wrote in this space about 3/4-inch crevices in the soil and the urgent need for watering trees and shrubs. The turnabout feels like walking through a doorway that separates the desert from the jungle.

My attitude towards gardening — and I'm sure yours, too — has done an about-face in recent weeks. Sweltering heat and hoards of mosquitoes make weed pulling and flower picking much less enjoyable.

What problems does "monsoon season" present to gardeners? Plenty, according to horticulture experts at the University of Minnesota and phone calls I've been receiving.

Saturated soil puts trees at risk of tipping from any wind that exceeds breeze intensity. Dr. Peter Bedker, Dial U extension forester and plant pathologist, says Colorado Blue, Norway and white spruce are particularly susceptible to tipping because of their shallow root systems.

If your spruce or other trees are leaning due to recent wet and windy conditions, Bedker says you can pull them back to an upright position if their trunk diameter does not exceed four inches or — for larger trees — if they're not leaning more than 20° from upright.

"When you pull a larger tree upright after it's blown over, it generally will not return to a healthy state because too many of its woody roots will have been severed," Bedker says. "Most trees simply cannot regenerate their larger woody roots and are prone to failure in the future." Bedker says it's generally better to remove these trees and start over with new ones.

What about staking trees as a preventive measure against future storms? Bedker says this is kind of like buying insurance — you may or may not realize the benefit later. "Personally, I am not staking the trees in my yard," he offered.

One reason trees tip, according to Bedker, is that they were doomed to tipping from the day they were planted because of the way they were grown in the nursery. Homeowners often unintentionally plant trees too deep, in other words.

It's a common nursery practice, according to Bedker, to purposely push soil around the base of trees during cultivation to discourage weed growth. Later, when trees are mechanically potted or balled and burlapped, this added soil is not removed. As a result, several inches of soil have been added above the root collar (the point where branch roots begin flaring sideways). Homeowners who plant these trees often simply drop the root ball into the ground and shovel a little more soil on top for good measure. Then, if the tree settles, it ends up in your yard stuck in soil 6 - 8 inches above the root collar.

These deep-planted trees are far more susceptible to being snapped off at ground level from heavy wind because the roots never got started correctly in the first place. Girdling roots may form just below the surface, literally strangling the stem and causing collar rot.

Best advice when planting new trees is to unwrap the burlap and dig away soil at the top of the ball until you uncover the root collar. Never plant trees deeper than the distance from the root collar flare to the bottom of the soil ball. The root collar flare should be at or slightly above grade.

One other rain-caused problem in trees and shrubs is fire blight. Mountain ash, apple, crab apple, cotoneaster and raspberry are most susceptible to fire blight, which is characterized by sudden wilting and dying of branches or the entire tree. Dial U reports they've received many fire blight calls in recent weeks. Fire blight is caused by a bacteria that can actually be forced into leaves by heavy rains. If you notice sudden wilting on branches of any of the trees and shrubs listed above, you should remove the infected tissue immediately by cutting out the branches at least 10 inches beyond the wilted tissue, destroying the infected tissue, and disinfecting your shears in a 10% bleach solution between every cut.

Does six weeks of drought followed by a month-long monsoon kind of make you wonder what's coming next? I'm not predicting snow in August, but some oddsmakers may just be willing to take that bet.

Lessons I've learned about gardening in 1997

Golf ball size hail is very hard on tomato plants, hosta leaves, blooming delphiniums and budding lilies. The white ice stones that sliced through the evening sky July 1 stripped off tomato leaves, blossoms and fruit, and ripped hosta leaves ragged. The beautiful 10-inch leaves on my two Francis Williams hostas will not likely return to their early summer grandeur.

The timing on starting seeds indoors in late winter is critical to summer success. Next year I'll start my begonias as early as January, and geraniums by the beginning of February. My geraniums started from seed never bloom until July and yet the geraniums at garden centers are blooming in mid-May. How come? The professionals must either employ some magic potions or start them very early.

Perennials are a long-term proposition. Many perennials don't reach their peak for 3 or 4 years, and even then they often need to be moved to provide more or less sun, wetter or dryer soil, or to give them or neighboring plants more room.

Hanging baskets require an incredible amount of water, especially during hot, dry, windy days. I have pots of petunias that need water every day. Potted plants will also perform much better if you give them a dose of liquid fertilizer at least once every two weeks.

Bad soil doesn't improve on its own. The best advice I can give to new gardeners is to make sure the soil is right before planting anything. My two best garden beds began with a lot of sweat. In one, I removed 17 wheelbarrows of clay and replaced it with humus-rich black loam. The other is a raised bed made of timbers into which I dumped a couple of cubic yards of rich soil. If your best efforts to grow flowers or vegetables never seem to break through into bounty and beauty, consider a complete soil overhaul.

Attempting to grow plants under a mature basswood tree is kind of stupid. My basswood is next to the driveway in my front yard, so naturally I'd like to show off dazzling colors, shapes and textures. Unfortunately, the maze of roots from this big old tree sucks the ground dry of moisture and other nutrients, and my plants end up "playing second fiddle."

Native perennials should be introduced into flower beds very cautiously. If wild flowers grow profusely in the woods or meadows next to your house, they will most likely grow profusely in your flower bed, much to the detriment of all the other stuff you want to show off in the same space.

Two examples from my yard are golden rod and wild violets. If you introduce a golden rod or two for late season color this year, you can expect a forest of golden rod in the same space next year. And wild violets...give them an inch and they'll take a mile. I have wild violets growing everywhere. Well, I guess they're better than thistles.

I've written before about my fondness for petunias. I've grown Purple Wave petunias the last several years. This year, I ordered several packages of Pink Wave, a newer, spreading variety said to be even more delightful than Purple Wave. It is! The other petunia I started from seed is Celebrity Chiffon Morn, a prolific bloomer with 2-inch creamy pink flowers. I mixed all three varieties in varying combinations in more than a dozen hanging baskets and the results have been fantastic.

Another benefit of starting these very showy — as well as pricey — petunias from seed is the fun and ease of giving them away as gifts during May and June. I gave my nephew a potted Purple Wave petunia as a graduation present and he showed it to me last weekend — it has dozens of cascading blooms and he may just become a gardener because of it!

Well, that's my partial list of lessons I've learned about gardening this year. Hope you're having an equally educational summer, horticulturally speaking.

Flowers on a mound?
Maybe...if you follow the rules

I recently attended a party at the Lakeville home of friends. The evening's entertainment included a frisbee-golf tournament around our host's wooded 20-acre lot.

One of my errant frisbee tosses landed in the host's beautiful perennial garden, a two-stroke penalty! While retrieving the frisbee, I paused to marvel at the stunning monarda, phlox, lilies, echinacea, sedum and other perennials.

"What's your secret to such beautiful flowers?" I asked the host.

"Part of it's location," she responded. "That entire garden is on top of our mound septic system."

Wow, I thought. My septic mound is planted to fescue grass and is about as exciting as a gravel road. My Lakeville friend's mound looks like a cover photo from Better Homes and Gardens.

I seeded my mound to grass because that was the recommendation of the contractor that installed the system. I didn't think I had a choice in the matter. Since a mound septic system can represent an investment approaching $10,000, the decision of what to plant on the mound really comes down to a question of maintaining the integrity of the septic system. Remember, the purpose of this space is to process and redistribute your household's waste water. When it quits working, life gets complicated.

To find answers, I talked with Mark Wespetal, a hydrologist with the Minnesota Pollution Control Agency. Interestingly, he said, the state has recently broadened its guidelines for mound maintenance. The new guidelines specify that any plant material should meet four criteria:

1. Protect against erosion. With a 4 to 1 slope, you want plants whose roots cling to soil particles in a heavy rain. This is why grass is such a good cover crop for a mound.

2. Frost protection. Plants should be capable of trapping winter snow that insulates the mound from deep freezing. Most short-lived annuals would not be up to this task.

3. No water-loving vegetation. You don't want plants that like to go deep for water, since roots can raise havoc with rocks and pipes in the mound. This rules out trees, shrubs and other deep-rooted plants.

4. No edible plants. This eliminates herbs and vegetable crops such as potatoes, carrots, tomatoes, beets and radishes.

The new guidelines clearly give us more flexibility than the earlier grass-only guideline, but they also raise our responsibility for maintaining the integrity of the mound.

So far, I haven't begun digging in any perennials. I'm still thinking about it. Have any of you had gardening experiences, good or bad, on your mound system? Let me know, and I'll share your ideas and experiences in a future column.

For those of you who start annual flowers indoors from seed in late winter, here's some new stars to look for in the seed catalogs: *Gypsophila muralis* 'Gypsy,' a compact baby's breath (10-14 inches) with a "loose, airy, casual or 'cottage garden' look;" *Celosia cristata* 'Prestige Scarlet,' a 15-20 inch celosia with numerous side-flowering branches; and *Zinnia angustifolia* 'Crystal White,' a compact (4-5 inches) zinnia with pure white, season-long blooms.

❖

Pumpkin update: I had carried about all the water my weary arms could handle when the rains finally came. Two rains of 0.6 inches in early August, and another 1.3 inch downpour August 10, made my plants lift their leaves in gratitude. I've got about 10 pumpkins in all, with the largest measuring nearly 2 feet in diameter. Now the question is, will the pumpkins reach maturity and stop growing soon, or will one of them truly become "the mother of all pumpkins?"

Trip to East Coast highlighted by historic garden tours

When I travel for business or pleasure, I always have my antennae up for nearby gardens. On a recent trip to the East Coast, I visited several gardens that were well worth the time and expense.

Longwood Gardens at Kennett Square, Pennsylvania (30 miles west of Philadelphia) is worth a visit even if this is your only destination. Longwood Gardens describes itself as "the world's premier horticultural display...a celebration of horticulture, architecture, music and theater." That's an ambitious moniker to live up to, but I'll be the first to admit that this is an impressive display.

Longwood's history dates from 1700 when the property was sold to the Peirce family by fellow Quaker William Penn. In 1798, brothers Samuel and Joshua Peirce began collecting and planting trees in a small arboretum that became known as Peirce's Park. Pierre du Pont (recognize that name?) bought the property in 1906 to save the trees because they were about to be cut for lumber.

Pierre S. du Pont, chairman of the DuPont and General Motors companies, was Longwood's owner and architect. As he developed the property, he continued the Peirce tradition of welcoming the public to share its beauty. After his death, he left the gardens "for the sole use of the public for purposes of exhibition, instruction, education and enjoyment."

Today, Longwood Gardens, Inc. is a private not-for-profit organization with 54 gardeners and hundreds of volunteers who tend to the garden's 1,050 acres.

A highlight of my visit to Longwood was a walking tour of the garden's heritage trees — some of the oldest and most majestic in the country. Many of these trees have reached heights of more than 100 feet. The collection includes many specimen trees familiar to Minnesotans, such as Ohio buckeye, sugar maple and little leaf linden, as well as numerous trees that we don't see growing in this part of the U.S.

The unusual bark of the London plane tree (Platanus x acerifolia) caught my eye. Plane trees tower to heights of more than 100 feet and attract the eye because of their exfoliating bark. As the plane tree sheds foot-long sections of bark, the trunk takes on a colorful, blotchy appearance of olive green, brown, cream and other color tones.

Longwood also has a cluster of four very old weeping hemlocks that have grown together to form one large cascading mound of foliage that is more than 75 feet in diameter. As I crawled inside this cavernous hideaway, the worn footpaths and pop caps evinced that other tree lovers had found their way inside over the decades, too. I'd love to have a similar hemlock mound in my yard but I don't think I can wait the 75 or 100 years it would take for the hemlocks to attain the shape of Longwood's planting.

My wife and I also visited Hampton Gardens on the north side of Baltimore. Hampton Gardens is a national historic site and includes a mansion built in the 1700s by Captain Charles Ridgely. His nephew, Charles Carnan Ridgely, governor of Maryland from 1815-1818, inherited the property in 1790 and set out to make the mansion and grounds a showplace.

In 1799, Charles Carnan Ridgely had 10,590 feet of wooden irrigation pipe laid to convey water from nearby springs to the mansion, gardens and meadows. By 1880, the gardens boasted over 20,000 bedding plants and 4,000 roses in more than 275 beds. By 1859, irrigation water was conducted from a spring by 2,000 feet of lead pipe to a reservoir at the mansion. From there, the system radiated to hydrants placed throughout the gardens.

Hampton Gardens has an impressive collection of mature native and exotic trees, several of which date to the early 1800s. One of the largest Cedars of Lebanon in the U.S. is located here and is believed to have been transported in the early 1800s from the Middle East in a shoe box. Three gnarled catalpa trees of the same vintage are still standing.

The largest saucer magnolia tree in Maryland was said to be an innovative hybrid when planted in the 1820s. The tallest tree on the property, at 115 feet, is a pecan tree.

A trip to the East Coast makes one realize how much more recorded history exists there than in the Midwest. As I stood outside Paul Revere's house in Boston, where Paul raised 16 children, I couldn't help think how Americans were busy working and playing and planting gardens on this street more than 100 years prior to the first settlers taking up residence in Minnesota.

My gardening advice, as a result of this trip, is to check out and visit the many wonderful gardens that exist in the places you travel to in the years ahead.

Autumn

Bring back forgotten sport of 'batting corncobs'

I can't get too excited about the baseball stadium controversy. Most arguments always seem to stop short of actually contemplating what we'd do with our lives if Carl moves the team to Charlotte.

Have you thought deeply about the quality of your life without the Twins?

I have.

It would give us an opportunity to evaluate some forgotten sports that thrived in these parts prior to ESPN and before Calvin Griffith moved the Senators to town from Washington, D.C.

One sport we might consider bringing back is batting corncobs. For a brief period during the fifties, the game flourished by offering plenty of spectacular pitches and electrifying hits. I know, because I was there, playing the role of designated hitter long before the DH became the American League rule.

The game was played most summer days as time allowed between more urgent jobs on our southern Carver County dairy and turkey farm. On National League game days, the Cincinnati Reds (Jim's team) played the Pittsburgh Pirates (Larry's team). On American League days, it was Jim's Detroit Tigers vs. Larry's Cleveland Indians.

Batting corncobs was an ingenious blend of sport, science and art. The game was just gaining momentum, and might have given Calvin a run for his money, when a development occurred in U.S. agriculture that relegated batting corncobs to a fate not unlike that of kerosene lamps and home canning.

What happened was that we lost our supply of cobs.

Forty years ago, most farm yards had at least one pile of

corncobs. Today you may have to drive across half a county just to find a pile.

The corncob's demise was brought on by the introduction of the cornhead attachment to the grain combine. These machines automatically shelled corn in the field and dropped the lowly corncob back to the earth to decompose. Initially two-row contraptions, the machines quickly grew to 3-row, 4-row, 6-row, 8-row and — I suppose somewhere in the Midwest — 12-row behemoths.

Prior to the combine, the entire ear of corn was hauled from the field and stored in wooden or wire corn cribs for later use.

On our farm, ear corn was stored in cribs in the fall and then ground in winter for dairy cows or stored until summer and fed to turkeys.

Like most farmers, we did not own a corn sheller. The task was farmed out to a custom sheller who arrived at the farm with his Rube Goldberg contraption that sent shelled corn one way, corn husks another and cobs out the back onto a giant pile.

The rules of batting corncobs were similar to the rules of baseball except that nobody actually ran bases; rather, carefully measured stakes in the ground indicated whether a hit was a single, double, triple or homerun. All runners had to be forced to advance.

The thing that made this game such a thriller was the pitch. A correctly pitched corncob was true art. Held crossways in the palm of the hand against a folded thumb, a hurled corncob could leave the pitcher's hand on a trajectory 4 or 5 feet behind a right-handed batter, then "break" (curve) left suddenly a few feet in front of the batter and cross the plate for a strike.

The pitcher (i.e., brothers Jim and Larry) could also deliver cobs that broke just as suddenly up, down or right. Now and then a "fastball" was mixed in to keep the batter guessing.

A cob that broke apart on contact with the bat didn't count. Jim recalls that lighter colored cobs stayed intact better than red cobs.

More blending of science and art went into bat construction. After one of us experienced a batting slump, we'd retreat into the workshop, then proudly emerge several hours later with a new bat sawn and sanded out of elm or ash that measured precisely 3 ft. x 1-1/2 in. x 1 in.

Since the game was never played before an audience, I have no way of knowing whether batting corncobs would have the crowd appeal of baseball. Judging by attendance at recent Minnesota pro sports events, batting corncobs might be just the boost that's needed on the local sports scene.

One obstacle to bringing back the game of batting corncobs would be finding a source of cobs. Farmers would have to give up their combines. My guess, however, is that, at a price of, say, $10 per bushel, we wouldn't have any trouble finding reliable corncob suppliers.

Phone call from Genevieve rewards volunteer

Someone once told me that the word "volunteer" doesn't translate into the Russian language. The concept doesn't exist in that culture. That's a sad commentary, because volunteerism is one of the cornerstones that supports our U.S. culture. Perhaps, since the breakup of the Soviet Union, things are now changing in Russia.

Every time a volunteer act occurs, it benefits at least two people — the person(s) on the receiving end, and the person doing the volunteering. Too often, when we're searching for volunteers, we undervalue the benefit that accrues to the volunteer.

I volunteer time as a Master Gardener because it makes my life more interesting. I write this column and answer phone questions about trees and other gardening stuff on a volunteer basis.

What's the point? Well, if I didn't do these things, I wouldn't have received the phone call last week from Genevieve.

Genevieve called me for advice about what type of tree to plant to attract birds. We chatted for awhile about choices and alternatives, and then she recalled that she had read one of my columns and enjoyed it. Also, she remarked, my name was somewhat familiar...what was my background?

I explained where I lived, that my name may be familiar because it's the same as my father's (a former county commissioner), and I explained how I came to be a Carver/Scott Master Gardener. Turns out my house sits on ground that is just a short walk from where Genevieve began her life more than eight decades ago. She recalls my home site in earlier years as a bucolic cow pasture.

I found her recollections quite interesting, since I've speculated that the soil on my lot has never been broken with a plow. A major clue is several big old bur oak trees that very likely pre-date the arrival of settlers to Carver County. That would mean, Genevieve reasoned, that the bur oaks were standing before 1862 — the year when much of Carver County was settled by recipients of U.S. land grants.

A little more conversation revealed that Genevieve attended Carver High School with my mother in the late 1920s. "Is your mother still alive and well?" she asked. She sure is, I offered, and suggested she give mom a call. "I'd like that," Genevieve said.

Genevieve said she continues to enjoy gardening. In fact, a friend used to tell her she had the nicest garden in Cologne. I could have predicted it, based on the fact that she's researching which trees to plant in her yard for enjoyment "in the years ahead."

Milkweed juice for warts, columbine for head lice

When I was a boy, I had warts on my left hand. Someone told me I could get rid of them by applying the juice from common milkweed. I tried it and it worked. It's one of those wonders of nature that, sadly, has largely passed from the common-sense knowledge we pass along from one generation to the next.

Today, it seems, most of us are more likely to race to Target the minute our nose runs or our stomach bubbles. Healing ourselves with plants growing just beyond our doorstep is becoming a lost art, driven from our culture in part by high-tech medicine and the media-driven marketing muscle of the pharmaceutical industry.

Native Americans used plants to cure countless ailments, and their cures were retained when the oldest generation passed on. Presumably, a wise tribal elder passed along his healing secrets to other tribal leaders before he passed along himself.

How many of us know how to heal ourselves using extracts or poultices from plants growing in abundance behind our lot, in the road ditch or down by the creek?

I picked up a book last week titled "Medicinal Plants," and was amazed to discover how many everyday ailments are treatable using common plants from our gardens or a few steps beyond.

Sure enough, the book suggests that milk from common milkweed does, indeed, cure warts.

I've written in this column before that the juice from plantain lily is an antidote for poison ivy. I am living proof that it works. Turns out that many plants can be used to reduce the irritation of poison ivy, including Canada thistle, yellow jeweled touch-me-not, yellow giant hyssop, wild lettuce, soapwort, horse nettle, white oak, white willow and Virginia Creeper.

The book lists many other fascinating treatments. Seeds from columbine can be rubbed into hair to control head lice. Chippewa Indians used root bark tea from Serviceberry (with other herbs) as a tonic for excessive menstrual bleeding. Along that line, 65 different plants are listed as remedies for "female" ailments!

Perhaps the most amazing plant, from a healing standpoint, is *Echinacea* — you may know it as coneflower. Plains Indians are said to have used *Echinacea* for more medicinal purposes than any other plant group.

The root (chewed, or in tea) was used for snake and spider bites, cancers, toothaches, burns, hard-to-heal sores and wounds, flu and colds.

Science has confirmed many of the traditional uses of *Echinacea*, plus cortisone-like activity and insecticidal, bactericidal and immunostimulant activities.

In Germany, more than 200 pharmaceutical preparations are made from *Echinacea* plants, including extracts, salves and tinctures. The plant is used for wounds, herpes sores, canker sores, throat infections, and as a preventative for influenza and colds. It is also a folk remedy for brown recluse spider bites.

Buying firewood confusing game for first-timers

Ever been here...you're at someone's home for dinner, and the hosts have a perfect fire burning in the fireplace? Before long, someone — usually one of the men — innocently asks the host, "Say, Bill, where do you get your firewood?"

Usually that one simple question launches a lengthy litany of facts and fiction about firewood. Happens every year about this time. I've been at that dinner party dozens of times. The questions are always the same...what kind of wood is it? What did they charge you? Is it a real cord, a fireplace cord, or a rick? How does it burn?

A common area of confusion has to do with measuring quantities. Since the sale and delivery of wood is generally not regulated, many a woodburner has accepted delivery of a mess of wood, only to discover long after the check's been written and the truck has wheeled away that the actual quantity is less than they thought they were buying, or the quality is not what was expected.

Consider the many ways wood can be sold — by the truckload, by weight, in ricks, runs or units, and of course by the cord — standard long cord, stove wood cord, short cord, face cord, or running cord. Is it any wonder that folks get confused?

Wood is generally sold in divisions of a standard cord — i.e., a neatly stacked pile 8 ft. long x 4 ft. wide x 4 ft. high covering 128 cu. ft. Since a stack of wood contains airspace, only 60-110 of the 128 cu. ft. may be solid wood. Usually it runs between 80-90 cu. ft., with round-cut wood containing more solid wood content than split.

Few people have 4 ft. fireplaces or stoves, and many lack the equipment to reduce 4 ft. lengths to stove dimensions. Therefore, wood is usually sold in face cords — lengths corresponding to either fireplace dimension (16 - 24 in.) or stove dimension (12 - 16 in.). When you buy a face cord, you are buying a pile 8 ft. x 4 ft. x whatever length dimension you specify. A rick (also called a "fireplace cord" by some) usually refers to 16 in. lengths.

The most common types of wood burned in this area are oak, ash, maple, and birch. In terms of actual energy value, here — in descending order— are the most dense woods, the woods that produce the most heat. (The numbers in parentheses are fuel value/cord in millions of BTUs). Shagbark hickory (30.8), white oak (30.8), sugar maple (29.7), American beech (28.0), red oak (28.0), yellow birch (27.3), white ash (25.9), American elm (23.8), red maple (23.8), paper birch (23.8), black cherry (23.1), Douglas fir (21.4), eastern white pine (15.8) and aspen (12.5).

One of the most disappointing mistakes a woodburner makes is buying wood that isn't sufficiently dry. Air-dried wood contains about 20-25% moisture. You can tell it's dry if the ends look weathered and contain cracks that radiate like spokes out from the heartwood.

Green wood, which is almost twice as heavy as dry wood, can be used to dampen an excessively hot fire or used at night to help hold the fire over. It tends to smoke more than dry wood and therefore increases creosote deposits and soot.

If you must burn green wood, the best choice is ash, since its moisture is relatively low on the stump. That must have been what motivated an anonymous English poet to write these words:

Beechwood fires are bright and clear
If the logs are kept a year.
Chestnut only good, they say,
If for long 'tis laid away.
But ash new or ash old
Is fit for queen with crown of gold.

Birch and fir logs burn too fast,
Blaze up bright and do not last.
It is by the Irish said
Hawthorn bakes the sweetest bread.

Elm wood burns like churchyard mold,
E'en the very flames are cold.
But ash green or ash brown
Is fit for queen with golden crown.

Poplar gives a bitter smoke,
Fills your eyes and makes you choke.
Apple wood will scent your room
With an incense like perfume.
Oaken logs, if dry and old,
Keep away the winter's cold.
But ash wet or ash dry
A king shall warm his slippers by.

Walnut trees cause of greatest number of queries

Of the hundreds of gardening calls I receive each year, the plant most asked about is the walnut tree.

Questions range from planting walnuts as an investment, harvesting and drying nuts for food, husking and cracking the rock-hard shells, extracting the dyes, and concerns about the toxic "juglone" given off by the plant.

Walnut trees were cultivated in ancient Babylon. Petrified walnuts were found on the table at the Temple of Isis in Pompeii. The Greeks knew the tree as "Persian nut" and the Romans as "Jupiter's acorn."

Ever wonder why we call someone a "nut?" The head-like shape of the walnut led to the nineteenth century use of the word "nut" to mean head, and the accompanying "off one's nut" to mean crazy. Later, the expression "to use one's nut" referred to thinking, "nuts" came to mean cuckoo, which led to "nut case," and these people sometimes ended up in a "nut house."

The two species most familiar to Minnesotans are black walnut (*Juglans nigra*) and butternut (*Juglans cinerea*). Interestingly, nearly all packaged walnuts are English walnuts grown in California.

Black walnuts can grow to over 100 feet with a crown nearly as wide. They prefer deep, rich, moist soil and develop an extensive taproot that makes transplanting difficult.

Black walnut wood is harder than oak and extremely stable once seasoned. Historically, black walnut wood has been popular for furniture and was the wood of choice for gunstocks because of its resistance to warping. It's been the wood of war, supplying gunstocks for Revolutionary war muskets and Winchester repeating rifles used in the war on buffaloes. In World War I, black walnut wood was used for airplane propellers.

The extraordinary toughness of the black walnut shell is the major reason it has not had the commercial success of its English cousin. Separating the nut from its fleshy husk can be a challenge. Naturalist Euell Gibbons recommended stomping nuts wearing heavy boots, while some walnut growers drive their pickup trucks slowly back and forth over rows of nuts. Some years back the USDA suggested using corn shellers to remove husks.

Whatever your method of husking, beware of the dye in the husks. A Swiss naturalist visiting the American colonies wrote in 1751: "The green peel yields a black color which could not be got off the fingers in two or three weeks time, even though the hands were washed ever so much."

I remember storing walnuts and butternuts on the south-facing sloped roof of our granary. The fleshy green fruit (anatomically similar to peaches and plums) gradually shriveled and turned dark brown. If memory serves, our methods of husking and cracking involved hammers and the workshop vice. Whatever we didn't eat while cracking, mother added to cookies and other treats.

The butternut's name is most likely attributable to the kernel's high (60%) oil content. Settlers used butternuts to polish furniture and advised that "a single nut kernel is sufficient to thoroughly oil one walking stick."

The butternut's brown dye colored the uniforms of Confederate soldiers a tan closely akin to the modern khaki, which led the Yankees to nickname the troops "butternuts."

The brown pigment in black walnut is called juglone. Exuded into the environment, juglone is toxic to microorganisms, fungi, insects, fish and even some mammals. Sensitive species attempting to snuggle up to a walnut tree are soon afflicted by "walnut wilt" — an slick way of maintaining personal space.

The most sensitive plant seems to be tomato, but other plants that can be affected are alfalfa, apples, asparagus, chrysanthemums, honeysuckle, peonies, potatoes, rhododendrons and roses. Resistant plants include hollyhocks, bellflowers, bee balm, Jerusalem artichokes, snowdrops, grape hyacinths, weeping forsythia, Virginia creeper, begonias, marigolds and pansies.

If you've planted black walnut trees to pay for your retirement, plan to live a long time. A healthy walnut tree may stand for two or three centuries. The Colbert Ferry Walnut in Alabama marks the site of the ferry that connected the Natchez Trace with the Tennessee River. It still stands and has a girth of 14-1/2 feet and a height of 78 feet. The largest walnut tree in the U.S., towering more than 138 feet, is in California. Minnesota's largest black walnut is in Olmsted County and has a girth of 13-1/4 feet.

Imagine — not a single 'big tree' in Carver County!

Big trees have always fascinated me.

When my dad said to park a farm implement next to "the big elm," I knew precisely the spot he meant.

Since the beginning of civilization, people have used big trees to direct others to a destination — i.e., "...stay on that road 'til you get to the giant oak tree, then turn right."

Meg Hanisch, with the forestry division of the Minnesota Department of Natural Resources, sent me a list this week of Minnesota's biggest trees.

The list contains measurements for circumference (measured 4-1/2 feet above the ground), height and crown spread for 53 native tree species.

Minnesota's tallest tree is a 128-foot white spruce in Koochiching County. The tree with the broadest crown spread — 117 feet — is a silver maple near Hastings. And the tree with the biggest trunk is an eastern cottonwood in Rice County — a monstrous beast with a girth of 30.4 feet. Think about the size of this tree — five adults, standing in a circle with their arms spread full, couldn't link their hands around it!

Earlier this fall, my son Fletcher and I took the short hike to Itasca Park's two big trees — the state's largest red pine (also called Norway pine) and what used to be the state's largest white pine.

The red pine stands 120 feet tall, has a crown of 36 feet and a trunk circumference of 9 feet, 8 inches (it may also be the most photographed tree in Minnesota).

Itasca's white pine is more impressive, with a trunk circumference of 14 feet 5 inches, a height of 112 feet and a crown spread of 49 feet. Although the sign at the base of this white pine claims it is Minnesota's record, it's been bumped from first place among white pines by a 15-foot circumference, 115-foot tall specimen near Bowstring in Itasca County.

The DNR list includes some other impressive trees. It lists, for example, a black walnut tree in Olmsted County with a circumference of 13 feet, 3 inches and a crown of 110 feet. Imagine the value of this tree in terms of furniture or veneer.

Other native trees with huge circumferences include a basswood in Washington County measuring more than 15 feet, a northern white cedar in Koochiching County of more than 11 feet, a bur oak near St. Peter of just under 20 feet and a black willow in St. Paul of more than 23 feet.

Almost 20 years ago, my dad and I walked along the Minnesota River northeast of Kelly's Lake in southern Carver County and measured the circumference of a cottonwood tree at over 26 feet. Dad said he first measured this tree in the early '30s. Its circumference then was 21 feet. I haven't returned to the site but Dad said he looked for the tree several years ago and it wasn't there anymore — most likely a victim of the river bottom floods of a couple of years ago. Kind of sad, isn't it, that such a specimen might now be nothing more than a rotting snag in the Minnesota River? Or perhaps it's providing underwater cover for a state record catfish.

The DNR registry of biggest trees might not, in fact, list Minnesota's biggest trees, Hanisch says. All it lists, she points out, is Minnesota's *identified* biggest trees. "There are many unreported giants just waiting to be found," Hanisch believes.

Of the 53 biggest trees on the list, not one is in Carver County. That doesn't seem right, does it? I think we simply haven't done our jobs locating our big trees. In other words, as you set out on your hikes in the days ahead, pack along a tape measure and report your findings — let's get a Carver County tree added to Minnesota's Native Big Tree Registry!

Fresh salsa good weapon against mosquitoes

Some years back, Garrison Keillor did a hilarious "News from Lake Wobegon" sketch about the extremes gardeners go to in late summer to dispose of their excess zucchini. You wake up some morning, he said, and stacks of zucchini are blocking your back door. You never discover for sure who stacked them there, but often you have a strong suspicion.

That's how a lot of folks are feeling these days about tomatoes. Suddenly, they're everywhere. The other day I went out and filled most of a 5-gallon pail with tomatoes, and in a couple of days, it was like I had never harvested!

My vegetable garden contains three species: Tomatoes, peppers and pumpkins. I make this statement with complete humility: I've had a bountiful tomato and pepper crop (the pumpkins are another story). My six tomato plants are yielding approximately a dozen ripe fruit per day.

Each August, about the time I've given away all the tomatoes my friends will accept and the plump red fruit are piling up on my back steps and kitchen counter, I heed the "Call of the Wild Salsa" and gather together the ingredients for another batch of culinary nirvana.

Salsa is good in my book if it contains plenty of garlic and plenty of fresh coriander (cilantro). There are no secret ingredients in Cliff's Salsa, but it definitely requires garlic and cilantro. With the exception of tomatoes and peppers, I buy my salsa ingredients at the grocery store.

Here is my process for making incredible salsa. There's no need to cook anything to make this salsa — it tastes great served fresh. Also, you won't find my instructions nearly as tidy or precise as recipes outlined in cookbooks.

141

Step #1 — Into a large bowl, empty a 6-ounce can of tomato paste, 2 tablespoons of olive oil and 1 tablespoon of red or white wine vinegar.

Step #2 — Peel and quarter about six good sized tomatoes and remove all the seeds and juice. Toss the meaty sections into a food processor and puree for about 10 seconds, then pour into the bowl.

Step #3 — Peel two large onions, cut them into sections, puree and pour them into the bowl. I usually use at least one purple onion for color.

Step #4 — Remove seeds from two bell peppers (include a red bell pepper for color), cut into sections and puree.

Step #5 — Remove seeds from about six Jalapeno peppers and process. I started my peppers from seed and the variety mix included Anaheim TMR 23, Hungarian Wax, Jalapeno and Long Red Cayenne; I'll use some of each.

Step #6 — Process about half a bunch of fresh cilantro, get high inhaling the incredible aroma, and toss it into the bowl.

Step #7 — Press 4 or 5 large cloves of garlic (more if your family can handle it) into the bowl.

Step #8 — Grind in about a half teaspoon of pepper and salt.

Stir everything together for a couple of minutes and then let the ingredients fight it out for top billing. Drive to Cooper's and buy a big bag of corn chips. When you return home, dip a sturdy chip into the thick red mixture and slide it into your mouth. The sensation will be overwhelming.

Feel free to consume the entire bowl of salsa with chips if you like. But bear in mind that this salsa also has many other uses. Try pouring several spoonsful on fried eggs. Add it to sandwiches. Serve it with tacos. The flavor seems to improve in the refrigerator as the ingredients marinate.

Two things to avoid with this recipe: First, avoid rubbing your eyes with your fingers after you've sliced chili peppers — the oil (capsaicin) burns like fire. Wearing of rubber gloves is advised.

Second, avoid asking for a raise within 24 hours of eating your salsa – unless you've shared your salsa first with the other party. You'll radiate a certain aura as long as the salsa remains part of our diet. You'll also be quite offensive to mosquitoes.

Ornamental grasses add year-round variety to garden

Can you think of a plant that puts on its best show in winter? I'd cast my vote for ornamental grasses — they're about the hottest thing going in gardening.

I've been a fan of ornamental grasses for years, primarily because of several clumps of feather reedgrass (*Calamagrostis acutiflora* 'Karl Foerster') growing in my yard. This grass grows to 4-1/2 ft. and is topped with stiff straw-colored seed stems that dance in the winter breeze.

A couple of years ago, I planted a pot of giant miscanthus (*Miscanthus floridulus*) to hide a utility post in my front yard. Last year it grew to over 8 ft. tall but failed to produce its plumy seed heads. This year's late fall enabled my giant miscanthus to produce its showy plumes in late October. Its bamboo-like stems and seed fronds wave gracefully above the new blanket of snow.

There are more than 100 ornamental grass varieties that will perform satisfactorily in our Zone 4 gardens. During the growing season, ornamental grasses range in height from 6 inches to 14 feet or more. They can be used as accent plants, ground covers, screens, border edgings, or as companions with a wide range of flowering herbaceous plants.

Listen to these descriptive traits of various grasses: pink flowers, huge leaves, winter sound and movement, dense blue-green foliage, silver plumes, red fall foliage, reddish-purple flowers, bamboo-like stems, yellow and pink stripes on new foliage, and green foliage with horizontal yellow bands. Now, aren't you a little bit curious and anxious to try some of these in your garden?

We are fortunate to have a local ornamental grass expert in

our community. Mary Meyer, who heads up Minnesota's Master Gardener program, also conducts research on ornamental grasses at the Minnesota Landscape Arboretum. In fact, she's authored a booklet, "Ornamental Grasses for Cold Climates," that contains descriptions and colored photos of the best grasses for our area. It's modestly priced and available at the Arboretum bookstore.

The primary focus of Meyer's Arboretum grass research is the miscanthus family. The experimental planting, which is near parking lot 8 on the Arboretum's 3-mile drive, features more than 30 miscanthus varieties.

The purpose of Meyer's research is to observe which grasses are the most winter hardy, exhibit fewest insect and disease problems, provide multiple season interest, have the most interesting colors, and interact best with the wind to provide motion and sound.

Based on this year's evaluations, some of the miscanthus varieties you may want to shop for next spring include 'Sarabande' (variegated 3/8-inch leaf with white vein), 'Bitsy Ben' (cascading feathery leaves; looks like a rag doll); 'Juli' (tall, slender, like a ballerina), 'Klein Fontaene,' 'Zebrinus,' and 'Variegatus.'

Ornamental grasses are propagated from seed or division, and can be purchased from seed companies and garden stores. Most improved strains will not come true from seed and must be propagated from divisions.

Ornamental grasses tend to be either clump formers that increase in circumference each year and can be divided, or rhizomatous type that spread laterally at varying rates. You should know what type you're planting and choose the site carefully, since some rhizomatous varieties can spread as much as 15 feet per year!

Perhaps you've heard people call any tall ornamental grass "pampas grass." The only true pampas grass is *Cortaderia selloava*, which will not grow in our climate. Last March, I started pampas grass seeds that I had ordered and grew them under lights through May, then transplanted the seedlings outside in June. The spindly plants never grew beyond knee-high and were a complete disappointment. I now agree that pampas grass is not meant for Minnesota.

If you want to plant an ornamental grass in your garden, I'd recommend starting with one of the miscanthus varieties mentioned above. Most garden centers should have one or more of these varieties available in pots next spring.

An excellent way to learn more about ornamental grasses is the Internet. I typed "Ornamental grasses" in the search box of a popular search engine and got a listing of 68 separate web sites, many that feature color photos of individual ornamental grass varieties.

'Dangerous gang' threatening native plant communities

If you or I heard news that a dangerous gang had moved into our area and was threatening to destroy entire communities, we'd be justifiably alarmed.

The truth is, a dangerous gang has moved into our part of Minnesota and it is threatening some of our nicest communities...plant communities, that is.

The gang is made up of several species of non-native buckthorn, a single-trunk small tree that was introduced into North America from Europe and Asia in the 1700s. Many Minnesotans planted buckthorn as hedges in the 1930s until they discovered buckthorn was an alternative host of crown rust in oats.

Some of the plant communities that are being endangered include native cherry and gray dogwood.

Buckthorn is a threat because it is invasive and grows in large, spreading colonies that can quickly crowd out desirable shrubs and trees. Buckthorn can invade any yard because buckthorn berries containing four or five seeds are eaten by birds and the seeds are deposited wherever songbirds leave their droppings. Buckthorn seeds can remain viable in the ground without sprouting during dry years and sprout several years later when moist conditions return.

The two non-native buckthorn species of greatest concern are common buckthorn (*Rhamnus cathartica*) and Glossy Alder or Fen buckthorn (*Rhamnus frangula*).

Buckthorn can mature to a height of 20 feet and has dark green elliptical to oval-shaped leaves. The bark and leaves often resemble wild black cherry (*Prunus serotina*). Common buckthorn produces 1/4-inch black berries.

Buckthorn is often found invading woodlands near cherry trees. It is common for the green leaves of buckthorn to remain on the plant into early winter, which makes it easy to spot in late fall beneath the canopy of deciduous trees.

I recently discussed the buckthorn threat with Diana Bolander, a horticulturist with the Eagan forestry department. She explained that when buckthorn crowds out gray dogwood, it is a very real threat to robins.

"In the fall, robins like to eat large quantities of gray dogwood berries in preparation for their migration south," she said. "When dogwoods are crowded out by buckthorn, this important food supply of robins can be quickly eliminated."

Both Minneapolis and St. Paul have begun buckthorn eradication programs, Bolander said.

Common buckthorn's name comes from the terminal buds which resemble the hooves of deer and the small thorn found growing between the terminal buds on branches.

Glossy buckthorn has no thorns and its glossy leaves are narrower than common buckthorn. Some nurseries are now phasing out buckthorn because of its threat to native plant communities.

Bolander said buckthorn can be difficult to control once it has invaded native plant communities because its growth is always aggressive.

"Simply cutting it down results in vigorous resprouting if no other control measures are used," she said. "This is because the extra sunlight that reaches the ground after cutting a stand of buckthorn encourages many more buckthorn seeds in the ground to sprout."

Effective control requires an initial labor-intensive cutting and clearing process, followed by close monitoring. Both physical and chemical control are often necessary to eradicate buckthorn and the process can take up to five years, according to Bolander.

Physical control involves cutting all buckthorn stems or trunks as close to the ground as possible (since buds are located beneath the bark, and will sprout new growth from the left-behind stumps).

Chemical control involves using either Roundup or Rodeo

herbicides, depending on whether the buckthorn is located near or away from a body of water (Roundup cannot be used near lakes, ponds or streams).

If you know you have buckthorn growing on your property, I suggest that you either write to me for more detailed instructions on controlling buckthorn or contact a tree inspector or forester in your community. Effective control requires following a detailed and rather specific five-year plan for eradicating buckthorn and restoring native plant communities.

Greece and Turkey trip reveals many horticultural highlights

When I travel, I am always fascinated by the contrasts and similarities between plants and gardens in Minnesota and the places I visit. I just returned from a trip to Greece and Turkey that yielded more contrasts than similarities. Here are some of the horticultural and agricultural highlights from 17 days of touring:

Olive trees are everywhere — on hillsides, in valleys, road ditches, parks, next to churches, in towns and cities. Roots and trunks of some olive trees are hundreds of years old, we were told, but careful pruning keeps the trees productive and vigorous. Trees are loaded with ripening fruit that will be harvested in November and December.

Both countries were in the middle of cotton harvest. In Greece, combines are slowly replacing hand picking, while in Turkey, the entire crop — thousands of acres — is harvested by Gypsies. We saw many Gypsy camps and traveling caravans, and most fields had clusters of 10 or 15 hunched-over men, women and children stuffing cotton bolls into baskets and sacks.

Cornfields were few and far between. A very large sunflower harvest had just finished in Turkey. Hand-picked roma tomatoes were being hauled by donkey-drawn wagons to processing plants scattered throughout both countries.

Santorini Island in the Aegean Sea is noted for it's white-washed hillside villages. It was hard for me to stop clicking photos of the brilliant flowers growing in hanging baskets, patio pots and tiny backyard gardens. If only we could grow Bougainvillea like this — it cascades down walls, scrambles sideways across patios and explodes in a panorama of glorious

149

pinks and reds. More dazzling color is added from lantana, hibiscus, geranium, oleander, cotoneaster and many species beyond my capacity to identify.

In Istanbul, Turkey, we toured the interior of the most opulent palace of all time (Dolmabahce), but my interest was drawn to the beautiful grounds surrounding the palace. Luxuriant magnolia trees grow to more than 50 feet and nearly as wide; I would love to see these trees when they're in full-bloom.

I was fascinated by the plane tree (*Platanus orientalis*), a huge tree that the Greeks have always associated with the pursuit of wisdom. Its leaves resemble a maple but its most distinctive feature is the bark, which flakes off in segments, exposing white wood which turns green and later brown. The trunks, which can grow to 5 feet or more, resemble a camouflaged hunter's outfit right off the pages of a Cabela's catalog.

We visited ancient Troy in northwestern Turkey, site of the legendary 10-year siege by the Greeks that culminated with the deceptive entry into the city by Greek soldiers concealed inside the Trojan Horse. While our group studied the layered rock foundations of 12 civilizations, I marveled at exotic oak trees with 2-inch diameter shaggy acorns.

I remember being surprised many years ago by the pine forest that covers much of North Carolina. On this trip, I was again surprised by pine forests that blanket the hillsides of Greece and Turkey. My childhood perception that northern Minnesota is the exclusive home of pine trees has gradually given way to the reality that pines are common on every continent.

The topography and climate in Greece and Turkey is similar to central California. The sun shines most of the time and nurtures countless species of fruit and nut trees. We sampled whenever and wherever we had an opportunity, including almonds, pistachios, pomegranate, apples, apricots, grapes and raisins, raspberries, and of course, delicious white and red wine.

Perhaps the prettiest sight of the whole trip, however, was the stunning red leaves on the row of amur maples that greeted us as we drove in our driveway, safe and sound, back in good old Minnesota!

Have you prepared your garden for winter stress?

This is investment season in the garden — your investment of time now will pay dividends next spring. Here are some of the chores you might want to consider this week:

• Divide lilies, day lilies and hosta this fall if the clumps are large, and replant them in your garden's bare spots. Add some mulch after you've planted the clumps and these perennials will grow roots in their new environment for several weeks following early fall frosts.

• The next couple of weeks in September is an ideal time to plant trees and shrubs. You can find terrific bargains on many trees and shrubs in the fall because garden centers prefer to sell balled-and-burlap and container stock rather than over-winter it. Water newly planted trees and shrubs liberally when you plant them, and then about every week to 10 days if it continues to be dry. Don't drown them by watering more often than once a week.

Like perennials, trees and shrubs will continue building their root system following frost if you've mulched the base of the plant with several inches of wood chips or shredded bark.

• Aerate your lawn now, especially if your lawn is growing on compacted clay soil. Lawn aeration machines are available for rent in most towns. Leave the plugs lay on the ground and they will decompose and provide nutrients to your lawn's root system this fall and next spring.

• Later this fall, when sub-freezing temperatures become routine, it's time to cover perennials to protect them from winterkill. Few things are as disappointing to a gardener than realizing in May that a promising perennial failed to survive the frigid cold of January and February. Plants such as chrysanthemums, iris and hosta will survive winter if you've covered them properly in late fall.

First, be sure to choose winter-hardy perennials, and don't plant them in poorly drained locations where they could rot before developing strong root systems.

Most perennials can be protected adequately by placing 4 to 6 inches of loose mulch (e.g., straw, marsh hay, compost or pine needles) over the plant in mid to late October, after there is some frost in the ground. This mulch protects the "crowns" (growing points) and helps keep the ground frozen all winter.

Without mulch, the soil may thaw during warm winter weather. When it re-freezes, the soil heaves. This alternate thawing and freezing damages many perennials, especially very shallow-rooted ones.

You can remove the mulch toward the end of March or early April as the upper layers thaw (don't be in too much of a hurry next spring!).

• Prepare now for rodent, deer and rabbit damage. Last winter, I discovered almost too late that rabbits liked the taste of a newly planted Honeycrisp apple tree I planted last fall. They ate the outer layer of bark from about half the circumference of the tree before I noticed the damage and installed a collar of hardware cloth around the base of the tree. Fortunately, the tree survived and the nibbled bark is regenerating. My observation about rabbits is, if it's not made of metal or plastic, they'll eat it!

Several good plastic tube products are available ("Tubex" and "Supertube"), or you can purchase 1/4-inch or 1/2-inch hardware cloth and form it into a circle around the trunk. The tube should extend into the ground 1-2 inches and extend up at least 2 feet for rabbits and 4 or 5 feet for deer.

• Maples trees should be wrapped with tree wrap to help prevent bark splitting from the warm wintertime sun. Each day as the sun sets, the bark cools off very rapidly and can split. Wrap young maples now and remove the wrap again next spring.

1,000-pound pumpkin in '96? It's possible...

My brother won the bet...he grew a bigger pumpkin. Officially, his behemoth weighed in at 94.9 pounds. While not a world record, he believes it is the largest pumpkin grown this year in Section 7 of San Francisco Township.

My best efforts produced a nicely shaped beauty that weighed...well, let's just say it's a good thing our bet wasn't $1/pound on the weight differential.

A friend told me he heard a report on public radio last week that this year's heaviest pumpkin weighed more than 900 pounds. This report conflicts, however, with a Minnesota Department of Agriculture news release stating that the world's largest pumpkin grown in 1995 was 789 pounds at Port Elgin, Ontario.

Closer to home, Fred Muermann of Chetek, Wisc. won first place among pumpkin growers at the World Pumpkin Confederation Regional Weigh-Off in Byron, Minn. with a 515.5 pound pumpkin. Muermann was awarded $200 and a plaque for his efforts. Second place at the Byron competition went to Wayne Peters of Rochester, Minn. for a 336 pounder, and third place went to George Heyne of Rochester, with a 313 pounder.

Paul Hugunin, a marketing specialist with the Minnesota Department of Agriculture, believes this year's heat and high humidity may have put a lid on world-class weights from our region.

The biggest Chaska-area pumpkin I've heard about was grown by Laurie Anderson of Jonathon. A first-time pumpkin grower, Laurie says she planted Burpee Giant seed and had three gorgeous vines that produced three good-sized pumpkins.

Her largest, weighing 119.7 pounds, almost didn't survive

because her 6-year-old son rolled it down the hill! She plans to use seeds from this pumpkin to grow next year's crop, which she hopes will produce at least four mega-pumpkins.

Keys to growing big pumpkins, she says, include lots of watering and frequent words of encouragement. "I tried to pat each of them every day while weeding and give them lots of verbal support to keep packing on pounds."

Another Jonathon grower, Sue Sipper, used Atlantic Giant seed to grow a half dozen pumpkins over 50 pounds. As her pumpkins grew, a path developed next to her small garden plot as neighbors came by to visit and observe the garden's growth.

Sue says she reads everything she can find about growing pumpkins and next year hopes to produce at least one that exceeds 100 pounds.

If growing big pumpkins sounds like a challenge you'd like to take on next year, here are several tips to get you started. Plant seed outdoors about May 20, or start seed indoors in late April or early May. Set the plants out in late May in a sunny spot in well-tilled soil. Manure or compost added to the soil will stimulate growth. A complete fertilizer like 10-10-10 can be added to the soil before planting (2 pounds/100 sq. ft.).

As the vines grow, stake them down so they can't blow in the wind. Pumpkin vines will grow additional roots from the nodes on the vines, and these new roots will help deliver water and nutrients to the fruit (yes, pumpkins are a fruit).

Pumpkins need at least 1 inch of water from rain or irrigation per week. A mid-season application of a balanced fertilizer side-dressed at the rate of 1 pound for each 25 feet of row will provide additional nutrition.

This is a perfect time of year to dream about big pumpkins. Start dreaming now, and — who knows? — a year from now you might be pictured on the front page of your local newspaper with your arms lovingly wrapped around the world's first 1,000-pound pumpkin!

Plant your own kaleidoscope of fall color

I just returned from three days in the "north woods." From a vista atop the Itasca Park forest lookout tower, two lone red maples *(Acer rubrum)* literally jumped out of the still-green landscape. Just two lone trees, among millions, were sporting their intense red-orange fall coat of leaves. By the time you read this, that same tower vista will be full of yellows, reds and oranges as the northern deciduous forest nears its fall-color peak.

Often we drive hundreds of miles to view spectacular fall color. Did you ever think of transforming your own yard into a fall-color extravaganza? The right trees and shrubs, planted yet this fall, can delight the eye for years to come.

Maples offer some of the most intense fall color. Amur maple *(Acer ginella)* grows with multiple stems to a height of 15 to 20 feet. Fall leaf color is a brilliant orangy crimson. A hybrid maple *(Acer x fremanii)* combines the best traits of its parents — silver and red maple — and is very colorful. Best cultivar is "Autumn Blaze." "North Fire" is the most-red of the red maples *(Acer rubrum)*. Among sugar maples *(Acer saccharum)*, "Legacy" offers the most intense fall color.

In the white ash family *(Fraxinus americana)*, "Autumn Blaze" and "Autumn Purple" turn deep purple in the fall. Make sure you get a cultivar that's winter hardy. White ash grow to about 60 feet.

We don't have many pin oaks *(Quercus palustris)* in this area because they prefer a slightly acid soil. If the pH of your soil is below 7.0, a pin oak will grow fairly fast (to about 50 feet) and be an excellent lawn tree. Fall color is red-orange to russet.

Red oak *(Quercus rubra)* is another fast-growing oak that

sports orange to red fall leaves.

Serviceberry *(Amelanchier* species), also called Juneberry, is a large shrub or small tree that has masses of white flowers in early spring and excellent yellow-orange to red-purple fall color. Edible blue-black fruit ripens in mid summer and is readily eaten by birds as it matures. Plants can be pruned into single or multiple trunked small trees or grown as large shrubs. Serviceberry will tolerate shade. For most intense fall color, look for "Autumn Brilliance," "Princess Diana" or "Cole's Select."

Guess why the common name "Burning Bush" was given to *Euonymus alata*? If you guessed fall color, you're right. This large shrub grows to 12 feet and has unsurpassed fall color that ranges from vivid pink to bright red. Burning Bush has reddish fruit and interesting winged branches that add interest to the winter landscape.

American Highbush Cranberry *(Viburnum trilobum)* grows to about 12 feet and a width of 6 to 10 feet. Large 4-5 inch clusters of small white flowers are showy in the spring, and late-summer fruit turns bright red and remains on throughout the winter or until harvested by birds. The foliage of this shade-tolerant shrub turns bright red in the fall. Popular cultivars include "Alfredo," "Compactum," "Hahs" and "Wentworth."

Most of the dogwoods have attractive purple leaves in the fall. My favorite is Pagoda dogwood *(Cornus alternifolia)*, which grows to 15 feet and has deep-burgundy fall color. Pagoda dogwood has a unique horizontally layered branching structure which accounts for its common name. Its 3-4 inch flat clusters of small white flowers in spring are attractive, and small blue-black berries in summer attract birds. Pagoda, Gray and Redosier dogwood all thrive in full shade, although sunny sites are acceptable.

Virginia Creeper *(Parthenocissus quinquefolia)*, also known as Woodbine, is a fast-growing vine that fits nicely along a fence or stone wall. Its large leaves turn bright red in the fall. Englemann Ivy is a selection of Virginia Creeper that climbs with adhesive disks at the end of tendrils. Its leaves are slightly smaller and also turn bright red in the fall.

Larch *(Larix* species) is one of the few conifers that loses its foliage each year. Before dropping, needles turn a spectacular bright golden yellow in late fall.

Think of all the money you'll save by planting some of these selections in your yard — while others are chasing all over the country searching for fall color, you'll be relaxing on your deck enjoying your own private kaleidoscope of color.

Composting transforms yard wastes into useful soil

To most gardeners, "harvesting" connotes picking armfuls of squash, tomatoes, carrots or some other garden vegetable or fruit crop.

Recently, I "harvested" my first crop of compost and it was an even more satisfying experience than the many vegetable, fruit and flower harvests I've reaped over the years.

Shortly after I moved to a new home in Carver County in 1993, a three-man construction crew (my father, my son and I) built a two-compartment wood frame-and-wire cloth compost bin. Each compartment is 4-ft. square and 3-ft. high. Building the actual bin was a fun project in itself. For years, I have wanted to compost but — on the postage-stamp size lot at my Minneapolis home — I had neither sufficient room for a compost bin, nor sufficient "stuff" to put in it!

Shortly after my new compost bins were set in place, I began filling them with oak leaves (my house is surrounded by mature red and bur oaks), grass clippings (collected before I traded my city "bagging" mower for a recycler model), vegetable and fruit scraps and coffee grounds from the kitchen (we don't have a garbage disposal), and any other green or brown plant material I wanted to get rid of from my new home site.

Every couple of weeks, I used a 4-tine hay fork to turn over the bins' contents. I kept the more "mature" contents in the right compartment and added newer material to the left side.

Very little decomposition occurred during the winter months of 1993-94. But as spring turned to summer, the mixture of plant materials began responding to the rain, heat and humidity and gradually decomposed into a fragrant (in an earthy sort of way) pile of gardening potential.

Finally, in late September, I declared my first crop of compost "mature" and transferred it to two old 30-gallon garbage cans moved from the city and a half-dozen smaller containers.

What will I do with these eight containers of "potential," you ask? Good question.

I have already used a couple of the smaller containers of compost for planting two blueberry bushes. Compost is ideal for this application because blueberries require a low-pH (acidic) soil. My soil tends towards a neutral pH so I mixed up a planting mix of black dirt, peat moss and 50 pounds of compost to help the blueberries feel at home.

Another key use for the compost will come next spring when I transplant annuals and perennials to outdoor beds and pots. Compost is also ideal as an additive to garden soil and around the base of newly planted trees.

One fun aspect of composting is watching the transformation that takes place inside the bin. This fall, I filled both bins to capacity with leaves and other yard wastes. By next spring, the piles will have shrunk to less than a third of their current size. I'm sure the ratio of input to output must be at least 10:1 — you need to add a lot of "stuff," in other words, to produce a crop of compost.

If you don't presently compost your leaves and other yard wastes, I suggest you give it a try — it's a fun project, and you'll feel like your labors are well-rewarded when you "harvest" your first batch of natural, rich, healthy, organic compost.

For information on getting started with your own compost pile, pick up a brochure from your county extension office.

Ornamental annual vines nice addition to garden

Each year, Master Gardeners from around Minnesota plant and evaluate vegetables, herbs and other plants, and then report their observations to the Minnesota Extension Service.

The results are summarized each February by Jackie Smith, veteran Carver/Scott County Master Gardener. These findings, from her summary, might help you select just the right vine for your fence, trellis or arbor.

Vine seeds were planted indoors March 31 and transplanted to gardens May 26. The cloudy weather was unusually hard on plants, with none living up to its performance in sunnier years. Vines are listed in order of their overall ranking, first to last.

Malabar spinach *(Basella alba)* germinated and grew vigorously, but was the last to begin vining at 30 days after transplanting. This plant, which climbs by twining stems, was attractive for over three months. The small, pinkish blooms were insignificant, but the maroon stems and succulent, glossy, heart-shaped leaves were well liked.

Malabar spinach was rated tops for color, and several growers commented on its usefulness in flower arranging. Several also spoke favorably of its culinary uses. It is edible raw in salads, steamed or stir-fried.

Balloon vine *(Cardiospermum halicacabum)* has tiny, white blooms which appeared fairly early. Combined with the lacy, delicate leaves, they made a lovely show by the first of July.

The puffy green seed pods were the main attraction, but when they faded gradually to tan the effect was no longer pleasing. The total display lasted an average of 98 days, with the vine vigor receiving a second-place rating.

Seeds needed to be nicked before sowing, making balloon

vine a bit more difficult to get started. This vine uses bloom pedicels to wrap around wire or string, so it was rather late to start climbing, at about 20 days from transplanting.

Cup-and-saucer vine *(Cobaea scandens)* caused germination problems for many growers, and the bloom was delayed until late in the season. There is no doubt the cloudy weather adversely affected this vine, which generally performs much better. The attractive, medium-green, oval-shaped leaves have climbing tendrils on their tips. Testers rated this vine second for leaf attractiveness and third for vine vigor. Many growers never saw the royal purple flowers.

Canary creeper *(Tropaeolum pereginum)* was the quickest to start climbing at almost three days before the plants were set outside. This vine climbs by leaf petioles that wrap around twine or wire. The dainty, deeply lobed leaves were attractive early, but faded by mid-August. It was also the quickest to produce its yellow flowers at an average of 44 days from transplanting. However, the color was not popular, and one grower commented that the blooms looked like yellowed flowers.

The growers also evaluated cinnamon vine *(Dioscorea batatas)*, a perennial, so it did not bloom the first year from seed. The twining stems started climbing while still indoors and then took a long time to regain vigor after transplanting. The leathery, elongated, heart-shaped leaves ranked first for their early attractiveness, with the plants maintaining a desirable appearance for an average of 122 days. According to Jackie Smith, this vine blooms prolifically in its second year and can perfume an entire yard!

Choose the right tool for the job...or invent it yourself

I've learned several useful lessons about tools as I've journeyed through life.

First, a job is a lot easier when you use the proper tool.

Second, if the right tool is unavailable — or beyond your budget — figure out how to make it yourself.

I've often observed people trying to do a job using the wrong tool. It's frustrating to watch, and more frustrating for the person doing the work.

Recently, my wife and I were riding on one of those people-mover belts in an airport. A worker was standing at the end with a plastic-handled putty knife. He was trying to clean out the metal grate at the end of the belt but he was forced to stop each time someone came to the end of their ride. He was using the wrong tool for the job, and he had only seconds to do the job before having to step back to allow the next passenger to pass.

Last year, on a trip to Egypt, I was startled to see street maintenance workers using machetes to hack large branches off boulevard trees. Someone presumably had instructed the workers to prune the elegant trees and then sent them to the boulevard with improper tools. The result was depressing.

Several years ago, in another third-world country, I watched workers mixing cement for a new home using the ancient method of pouring water and cement into the center of a pile of sand. When the mixture was stirred to just the right consistency, the mix was removed from the center of the pile, and more water and cement were added to make the next batch. And so it went until the house was built. A cement mixer would have come in handy.

On a recent trip to South Carolina, I watched a hired garden worker remove last year's growth of ornamental grass by pulling one handful at a time with his fist and stuffing it into a 5-gallon pail. When the pail was filled (about ten handfuls), he carried it to a wheelbarrow, dumped the pail, and returned to the grass for more hand pulling.

Each of these workers could have done a better job, and enjoyed the work more, if he had selected (or been given) the right tools.

I probably learned the lesson of inventing tools from my father.

A while back, my siblings and I were cleaning out Dad's workshop and garage in preparation for an auction. As we scrounged through years of accumulated clutter, we kept discovering inventions Dad had fabricated to do jobs his existing tools weren't capable of.

Many of these devices were skillfully crafted from hardwood and were held together by bolts or screws.

A wood footstep attached to a tapered piece of white ash was designed to create slots in the ground for planting tree seedlings. Dad planted thousands of trees during his lifetime and the device saved time and labor.

An elongated wheelbarrow-shaped cart crafted out of a bicycle wheel and sturdy ash wood made hauling a deer carcass out of the woods easy work after a successful hunt.

A workshop lamp had several curious holes at the center of the stand. The dual-purpose lamp lighted the saw blade work area and the holes were drilled at just the right height to accommodate the vacuum hose that sucked away the sawdust.

Two hip-replacement surgeries and tired knees caused by years of milking cows led to Dad's ingenious scissors-like wooden "picker-uppers" and countless two-foot-long shoehorns that enabled him to don shoes without bending over.

The intended use for several of Dad's inventions defied comprehension. When we asked him for an explanation, he often replied with a smile, "I'm not sure what I had in mind when I made that."

So what, you might be asking, does all this have to do with gardening?

Well, for one thing, I think we're lucky that we have such a vast array of tools at our disposal. In fact, based on some of the gardening catalogs I receive, there are more tools available than there are applications.

Second, now and then we may find ourselves tackling a gardening project for which we don't have quite the right tool — or perhaps the right tool hasn't been invented. When faced with this situation, ask yourself if this your opportunity to invent the tool that thousands or maybe even millions of gardeners will stand in line to buy.

Think about what it could mean — instead of trying to squeeze a few minutes of gardening in here and there between your career and family responsibilities, you could begin living off the royalties of your invention and spend the rest of your life gardening. The next gardening "miracle tool" may be just an ingenious thought or two away.

About The Author

Cliff Johnson has been active in the University of Minnesota Extension Service Master Gardener program since 1993. He has written extensively on gardening topics and answers hundreds of phone calls each year about gardeners' tree and shrub problems. He serves on the Minnesota Master Gardener state advisory board.

Since 1986, Cliff has operated his own marketing consulting business. Previously, he worked in publishing, public relations and advertising. He has a degree in journalism from the University of Minnesota.

Cliff is married to Wanda and has has two adult children, Amber and Fletcher, and a granddaughter, Lily.

For questions or comments about this book or most any other subject, contact:

> Cliff Johnson
> Phone 612-466-2288
> Email Cliffmg@aol.com